Tales of a
Slightly Off

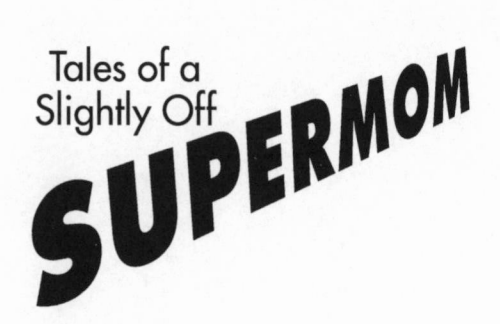
SUPERMOM

Tales of a Slightly Off

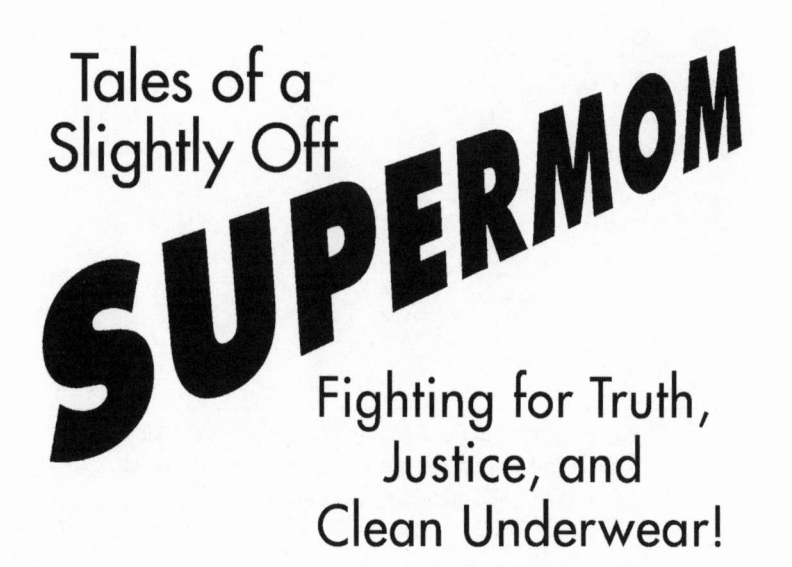

Fighting for Truth, Justice, and Clean Underwear!

By Deb DiSandro

PELICAN PUBLISHING COMPANY

Gretna 2003

In loving memory of my father, Jack Dempsey

*The word "Pelican" and the depiction of a pelican are trademarks
of Pelican Publishing Company, Inc., and are registered
in the U.S. Patent and Trademark Office.*

Library of Congress Cataloging-in-Publication Data

DiSandro, Deb.
  Tales of a slightly off supermom : fighting for truth, justice, and clean
underwear! / by Deb DiSandro.
    p. cm.
  ISBN 1-58980-070-2 (alk. paper)
  1. Mothers—Humor. 2. Motherhood—Humor. I. Title.
  PN6231.M68 D57 2003
  818'.707—dc21

2002009503

Printed in the United States of America

Published by Pelican Publishing Company, Inc.
1000 Burmaster Street, Gretna, Louisiana 70053

Contents

Acknowledgments

To my mother, Jean Podgornik, who believes I can do anything.

To my husband, Anthony, and my children, Marcus, Lauren, and Jenna, who enrich my life and gave me permission to share their stories.

To my family and friends, especially Diana Geldmyer, who is always there when I call to say, "How does this sound?"

To my writing mentors, Ellen Hunnicutt, Bill Nelson, and especially Marshall Cook, whose steadfast support helped me to see this project through.

To the Quintessential Writer's Group, especially Jane McCaffrey, who changed my creative editing into proper grammar.

To my comedy mentors, especially Jerry Rannow, who helped with the comedic timing of this book, and my dear friend, Dobie Maxwell, a funny man with a big heart, who thought I was funny enough to be on the radio.

Introduction

I believe it was esteemed author and poet William Shakespeare who once said, "All the world's a stage, and for parents, 'tis merely one darn stage after another!" Or maybe it was Shakespeare's mother.

Our little thespians first enter stage right mewling and puking. (If you threw out your high-school cliff notes, *mewling* means bawling like a baby, and if you don't know what puking is, you're not a parent.) Yes, it's the infant stage, when all we yearn for is to sleep and wake up when our kids can pay for their own Nikes.

Then it's onto the biting stage, which, unfortunately, some sportscasters and boxers never OUTGROW.

At about three, we wander through the I'll-Do-It-Myself stage, which arrives when they can't do anything themselves. So that by the time they finally get dressed in the morning, it's time for them to put on their pajamas.

Then at six or seven, they enter the You-Do-It-for-Me stage, which lasts until, oh, about fourty-two.

When your child's chief advisor sports an earring through his tongue and pants the size of France, you know you've arrived at the And-If-Your-Friend-Jumped-Off-a-Bridge-Would-You-Jump-Too? stage.

But most dazzling of all is when your talented actor throws a temper tantrum in the middle of Kmart. No, this is not the Terrible Twos, but an upgrade called the Terrible-Twos-for-Teenagers stage, which occurs when you refuse to buy them the CD with the parental-warning advisory.

Oh, woe is *we*! Our children strut and fret each hour of every stage until, alas, we, the weary parents, have had it up to our Elizabethan eyebrows. But, ultimately, are these stages merely much ado about nothing? It will take some time before we can tell—pray, tell—if "all's well that ends well."

Now, join slightly off supermom, Deb DiSandro, as she takes you through the many ages and stages of parenthood. Once you see how this supermom is able to balance it all, you'll breathe a deep sigh of relief and say, "Wow, and I thought my family was dysfunctional!"

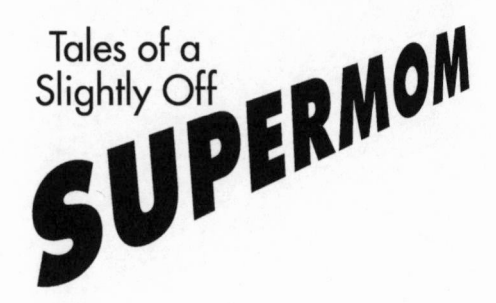

Tales of a
Slightly Off

SUPERMOM

CHAPTER 1

Battles Burps, Bottles, and Binkies

One of my friends told me she was in labor for 36 hours. I don't even want to do anything that feels good for 36 hours.
— Rita Rudner, stand-up comedian

BABY-TO-BE DELIVERS MORE THAN EXPECTED

(Scene: Inside maternity ward)

"The fetal monitor indicates that you're not in labor, Mrs. DiSandro."

"What do you mean I'm not in labor, doc? I'm extremely uncomfortable and today *is* my due date you know!"

"Well, it seems we may have miscalculated," the doctor explained. "Your baby is not due on July first, as we had previously thought."

"So how much longer? July second? Third? A Yankee Doodle baby, maybe?"

"You might want to sit down for this, Mrs. DiSandro," the doctor gently informed me. "You see," he began. "It's very possible. . . . Gee, I don't quite know how to say this . . . but you may be the first woman in history to be pregnant forever."

"Forever!"

"Yes, forever. We've run some extensive tests, and by all indications, your baby isn't . . . well, how can I say this, too thrilled about leaving the womb."

"What?!"

"It seems your baby-to-be would like to see a few things worked out before it's willing to enter the birth canal. He or she has given us quite a list."

"You've got to be kidding!"

"It's a new century, Mrs. DiSandro. Haven't you heard of children's rights?" (I suddenly had the feeling I'd been watching too many episodes of *Court TV* during my pregnancy.) "Your baby's first concern is about your, uh, level of communication."

"My level of communication? You can tell that kid I happen to have a college degree! Okay, it's only from a television school, but it's accredited—I think."

"To put it bluntly, you shout, especially when talking to the other two little people in your family. The baby figures if the shouting is this loud from the inside, the noise must be deafening on the outside. So he or she would like to see you tone things down a bit before arriving."

"But, but, it's summer and my children keep slamming the back door and telling me they have nothing to do, and it's 90 degrees, and I'm eight months, twenty-eight days, twenty-two hours, sixty minutes, and 4.3 seconds pregnant!"

"Oh, and about your eating habits," the doctor continued. "The baby is sick of all those nutritious snacks—carrots, cucumbers, fruit, and the occasional French fry you've been eating. Your baby insists that you add a little variety to your diet. Some suggestions were Hostess cupcakes, potato chips, Yoo-hoo chocolate sodas, and Klondike bars."

"Oh, really?"

"Yes, and he or she has repeatedly tried to tell you its preferences on no uncertain terms."

"I see. So you're saying most of the swift kicking and constant rib jabbing is intentional?"

"Exactly. And, another concern, the kid-to-be doesn't like how often you use the word "no.""

"Is that so?"

"Seems you frequently say no to snacks before meals, staying up late, new toys, and bungee jumping off bridges. So the baby would like you to practice saying 'yes' before it agrees to start effacing."

"Let me get this straight. If I say 'yes' to more toys, sugary snacks, and risky activities, the kid will start effacing?"

"Correct."

"And what will it take to get to three centimeters?"

"A new bike at age three and a half."

"And ten?"

"Tickets to Disney World at age five."

"I believe I've heard enough, doctor."

"But there are at least a dozen more stipulations, Mrs. DiSandro. Now if . . ."

"Give me that fetal microphone. OKAY, LISTEN UP MY GENIUS BABY-TO-BE! I'LL GIVE YOU FIVE MINUTES TO STOP YOUR WHINING AND START EFFACING. IF YOU'RE NOT OUT OF THERE WITHIN THE NEXT FOUR HOURS, I'LL GIVE YOU SOMETHING TO COMPLAIN ABOUT! AND IF YOU HAVE ANY PROBLEMS, I'LL JUST HAVE TO COME IN THERE AND GET YOU MYSELF. HAVE I MADE MYSELF PERFECTLY CLEAR?!"

"Mrs. DiSandro, this is astonishing! Your contractions are beginning to show up on the monitor. They're getting stronger and stronger! I believe you're in labor."

"It just takes a certain level of communication, doc."

(*Note:* Although I admit that this was just one of those pregnancy dreams, Jenna DiSandro was born on June 28, a few days before her due date.)

BABY GIVES BIRTH TO SECOND SET OF PARENTS

When a slight age gap separates your first baby from your last—say, for instance, ten years—the older child often assumes a new role. Suddenly, a deep furrow appears between his brows. He mopes around sighing and shaking his head and frequently crying about the cost of college tuition. He becomes a dad.

If the age gap between the second child and the last is, say, eight years, the second child starts ordering everyone around and saying, "I'm right! I'm right!" She becomes, well, a mother.

When we brought our new baby, Jenna, home from the hospital, we assumed we were her only parents. Until our son—new dad, Marcus (age ten)—asked, "Can we afford her?", and our middle child—new mom, Lauren (age eight)—shrieked, "Be careful of her soft spot!"

Having recently graduated with high honors from the hospital baby class, Jenna's two older siblings were heavily armed with information. They knew how to hold Jenna and support her head, feed her, rock her, and sing soft lullabies to soothe her newborn fears. Jenna bonded with them instantly.

For me, the other mother, it wasn't so easy.

"Can I feed Jenna this time?" I pleaded with the doting parents.

"Are you sure you know how?" Marcus inquired.

"Here, let me check the bottle," Lauren said, snatching it from my hands. She shook a few drops of formula onto her wrist. "Too warm."

"It's fine." I assured her. "Believe it or not, I actually raised two children without your help."

"Yeah, but that was a long, long time ago," Marcus informed me. "You're old now."

"I can manage," I assured him.

"Who showed you how to buckle Jenna's new car seat?" he reminded me.

"Me!" Lauren piped up.

"And who showed Daddy how to assemble that Exersaucer?" Lauren asked.

"Me!" Marcus chimed in.

"Now, why don't you go run this bottle under cold water for a few minutes," Lauren suggested while taking Jenna from my arms. "Then we'll talk about you feeding our baby."

"But she's my baby," I pouted.

Or was she?

Like a protective mother hen, Lauren tossed aside Dr. Seuss for Dr. Spock the first time Jenna sneezed. When Jenna cried, she'd flip to chapter six and cluck, "The poor thing has gas, mom. She needs to be burped. Hand her over."

A few months later, when Jenna learned to crawl, she'd scoot into the family room where Marcus was watching television with his friends. He'd quickly switch from *Goosebumps* to *Sesame Street*. "It's better for babies," he explained to his disgruntled buddies. "You'll understand when you have children of your own someday."

It's Marcus who checks the grocery-store ads for sales on baby formula and Lauren who reads the baby-food jars for added salt and sugar. It's Lauren who remembered the "Rubber Ducky" song for Jenna's first bath and Marcus who patiently taught her how to play patty-cake. Then he proudly showed his baby-less friends. They just rolled their eyes and said, "Marcus, get a life, man!"

The first things Jenna sees every morning are the bright faces of her brother and sister peeking over the side of her crib. Cooing and whispering, they let down the side of the crib, gently take her out, carry her into one of their bedrooms, and close the door. Giggles and kisses and goo goos are shared all around.

When Marcus and Lauren burst through the door after school, Jenna's face lights up, and she squeals with delight. For the rest of the afternoon, I'm invisible, as she crawls into their waiting arms.

From the safety of her Exersaucer, she watches them play board games with their friends. When they laugh, she laughs. When she cries, they cry. When she goes to bed, they squeeze her as if she'll be away forever.

Not every baby is lucky enough to have two sets of parents. At least, that's what I keep telling myself when Jenna wrestles out of my arms to fall into her sister's, or when she shoves a book in her brother's direction and he scoops her up onto his lap to tell her about the adventures of Tommy Tugboat.

I'm ecstatic about it. Really! I am. Honest.

Commotion from the family room breaks through my thoughts.

"Mom, come quick!" Marcus and Lauren shout. "Jenna NEEDS you!"

SHE NEEDS ME! MY BABY NEEDS ME! I rush into the room.

"Mama," Jenna says holding up her pudgy arms.

I pull her up and hold her to my chest. "Mommy's here, sweet pea," I coo. "Your mommy's . . . ugh . . . PEEEEUUUUUUU!"

"She dropped a big load," Marcus says.

"Don't forget to use salve so she doesn't get a rash," Lauren reminds me.

"I think I can handle it," I say, holding Jenna at arm length. After all, only real parents change dirty diapers.

SANDMAN, WE HAVE A PROBLEM!

As the parent of a toddler, creating conditions perfect for my little one's nightly trip into dreamland can be exhausting. While putting her to bed, I go through more checks and rechecks than a DC-10 preparing for takeoff. The three Bs—bath, book, and brushing—go smoothly enough, but we usually hit turbulence after depositing the passenger into her crib.

Pacifier in? Check.

"NO, Mom, not that facipier. The uver facipier!"

"This one?"

"Uh-uh," she shook her head.

Fasten your seat belts. We've hit a few bumps.

"How about this purple one?"

"Uh-uh," she pouted, shaking her head again.

"Okay, how about this gunky one with last night's meatloaf on it?"

"Yeah, dat one! Put the uver ones over there," Jenna says, pointing to her dresser.

"Okay. All the other facipi—uh, I mean, pacifiers are on your dresser."

Pacifier in? Check. Reclining baby into sleeping position . . . check.

"I need my blankie!" Jenna pops up.

Delay takeoff, control tower. Repeat. Delay takeoff. Missing blankie!

"Here it is."

Depositing blankie, ruffle side up, for easy scrunching . . . check.

"Uver blankie, too, mom."

"Two blankies?"

"Yeah."

"You'll be too hot."

"UVER BLANKIE, TOO, MOM!"

Positioning blankie number two, ruffle side up . . . check.

"Light on," Jenna demands.

Night-light on . . . check. Backing out of the room, backing . . . backing . . . backing out as I ease the door shut, saying "goodnight" sixty-seven times and "Mommy loves you" eighty-seven times. Door is closed . . . check.

Door secure! Prepare for takeoff! Listening . . . listening . . . listening outside the door.

Silence.

Tiptoeing toward the stairs . . . listening . . . listening.

Silence.

We're preparing for rapid eye movement. Halfway down the stairs, now . . . listening . . . listening.

Silence.

Okay, folks. I believe we are just seconds from maximum sleeping altitude! Reaching the bottom of the stairs, and . . .

"MAAAAAAA!"

Sandman, we have a problem. Aborting takeoff. I repeat. We're aborting takeoff. Heading back upstairs into room.

"What?"

"Um . . . mom, is Danielle seepin?"

Oops! Forgot romper-room check.

"Yes, Danielle's sleepin'; your cousins Mollie and Meghan are sleepin'; Barney's sleepin'; Big Bird's sleepin'; everybody in the whole wide world is sleepin', except you and me!"

Shut door . . . check.

"MAAAAA!"

"WHAT?? I mean, what is it now, darling?"

"Is it dark out?"

"Yes, it's dark out. See, I'll show you. Dark, dark, night, night."

Backing . . . backing . . .

"Mom, I'm scared! Sing me a song."

"A song, sure, a song. Let's see. How about 'Brahms' lullaby'? Go to sleep. Go to sleep, before I completely lose my mind . . . go to sleep . . .'"

"No, mom, sing 'Pump up the Jam.'"

"Pump up the *what*? I bet your big brother taught you that one."

Getting ready to call in the copilot: dad. Nix the copilot. He'd just sleepwalk into the room, scoop up the baby as if she were a sack of potatoes, and deposit her directly in the middle of our bed, which the baby will consider her nighttime party room for the next three hours, as she jumps, hops, and kicks her way to 4 A.M.

Reinstate rocking. Rocking . . . rocking . . . humming . . . rocking . . . rocking. Yawning . . . yawning . . . soft breathing . . . getting deeper . . . deeper . . . SLEEPING!!

WHACK!

"Ouch!"

"Wake up, mommy. Wake up!"

"Okay, okay, I give up. You win, Jenna. You can sleep in my bed—just this once. Do you hear me?"

"Kay, mom."

"Just this once!"

"Kay, mom, just like last night?"

"Yup (yawn), just like last night."

A McGAGGING EXPERIENCE

You may have noticed that pint-sized diners with a penchant for blowing bubbles in their milk and sticking peas up their noses have become common place in restaurants these days. Although it may seem their sole purpose for being there is to irritate you— the lucky, childless diner—nothing could be further from the truth.

Believe me. If the hostess had asked whether we preferred to sit next to the lady from the children-should-be-seen-and-not-heard school of parenting, or the family of ten juggling the salt and pepper shakers, ketchup bottle, and skinny waiter, we would have gladly opted for the circus act. Although my husband and I thoroughly enjoyed the stares and glares from the lady—who, due to selective memory, could only recall how wonderful her now-grown, no-longer-living-at-home children were as young-sters—our kids would've been better entertained by the sight of the terrified waiter flying through the air. And had we known that the first dinner roll would launch from my son's hands like a space shuttle and deflate the lady's bouffant hairdo ("Oh my gosh, I'm so sorry, ma'am. I swear it was an accident. He was aiming for his sister, but she's learned to duck"), we most certainly would have chosen to stay at home.

It all begins innocently enough, this naive notion to take three children to a sit-down restaurant. Just once, for old time's sake, you and your husband long to hear your server say something other than, "Pull up to the second window!" You yearn for a few more menu choices than "supersize it."

So you delude yourselves into thinking it would be a valuable experience for the kids to sit down and criticize someone else's food for a change. You convince each other that it couldn't be any more exhausting than eating at home, until you pull out of the driveway and the backseat harmonizers begins a rousing chorus of "I'm starving! I'm starving!"

Once at the restaurant, the delusion and denial continues:

"Twenty-minute wait? No problem."

"How many in your party?"

"Uh, four."

"But you have a toddler."

"That's right. We always forget about her. But she doesn't take up much room."

"Then you're not a party of four; you're a party of FIVE."

"Oh, no! Not a party of five! Now we'll never get seated!"

Two hours later, while seated at a table so small we had to keep our elbows on the table next to us, the kids began gnawing on the empty breadbasket as an appetizer. "Could we have some crackers, PLEASE?"

After the sixth basket of crackers, and after helping the older kids find the sixtieth word in the search-a-word puzzle on the children's menu, while convincing little Jenna to at least save the yellow crayon for dessert, our meals finally arrived. This is when my husband and I discovered the only thing you can count on at a sit-down restaurant: your children will most definitely not eat.

"What's that green stuff?

"Parsley."

"What's it doing on my plate?"

"It's a garnish."

"Eeewww! The garnish touched my burger! Gross! I can't eat it."

"Then eat your fries."

"They have black spots."

"It's called seasoning."

"I think I'm going to throw up."

"Are you enjoying your food?" the server asks as he cleans up our daughter's third cup of spilt milk.

"What food?" my husband asks.

"The food you're eating."

"Are we eating?" I replied. "I hadn't noticed."

On the way home, the chorus begins again: "I'm starving! I'm starving!"

We drive to the nearest drive-through.

"Pull up to the second window!" never sounded so sweet.

PASS THE PASSY, PLEASE!

My daughter is fast approaching her third birthday.

"You know what happens when you turn three?" I said, preparing her for the big event. "Of course, it doesn't have to be on the exact day of your birthday," I added, dreading the occasion myself. "The day after will be soon enough for one of the most traumatic experiences of your young life."

"What?" Jenna asked.

"No more passy. Three-year olds don't use pacifiers," I reluctantly informed her.

"Oh," she said while sucking on her passy and contentedly rubbing the threads of her ruffled blankie.

Since she has very little concept of time, the thought of giving up passy doesn't phase her right now. But it will. Oh yes, it will, which is why she still has a passy at three when all the experts say babies should give them up by nine months, or twelve months, or certainly by the age of two. And then there are those extreme antipassyists, who believe babies should never use pacifiers.

But none of these experts were around at three in the morning when my daughter wouldn't stop wailing. I know because I tried to call them!

I don't think it's any big deal. It's not like she's addicted to it or anything. Besides, my baby only uses her passy for bedtime. Honest! Okay, long car trips, too, which include any trip past the corner. But that's it, really! That, and the occasional video. Well, of course, when she gets a boo-boo, there's no question. And I wouldn't step foot in the mall without it. Oh, and if she misses her nap, well, who could blame . . . okay! I admit it. She's a crazed sucking passy-head! There, I said it.

But withdrawal is, like, so . . . hard! I remember when my first-born, Marcus, turned three. He bravely tossed his pacifier into the garbage can and went down for his nap without a single cry of protest. I was amazed at how easy it was. Had I known, I would've done it sooner.

But then the garbage truck rumbled up the block and my son crumbled to the floor in a quivering heap. "My Binky is gone forever!"

I suppose he thought that as long as the pacifier was in the garbage, he could always retrieve it if life got too tough. But the garbage truck crushed his hopes, along with his Binky. Ten years later, he still can't look at a garbage truck without whimpering.

Of course, the longer you wait, the more attention you draw to the situation. And enforcers from the pacifier patrol are sure to comment:

"What's a cute little girl like you doing with that thing in your mouth?"

"I can't understand you when you're sucking on that piece of plastic."

"That big plug covers your whole face. But it's not your fault; it's your mommy's fault."

It used to offend me, but that was before I discovered the truth. They're just jealous. They're suffering from "passy, envy." I know because I've felt it myself.

In the midst of one of those extremely stressful days, I glance over at my daughter sucking on her passy. She looks so relaxed, content, and sublime, like a little Buddha at one with her passy, that I can't help but think, "Boy, I could sure use a passy, right now!"

And why not? Maybe the passy, is wasted on the young?

Instead, adults should have passy bars, where they could stop for a quick passy break before heading home. A passy could get you through a traffic jam, your kid's piano recital, and that moment when the doctor tells you to turn your head and cough.

For taking the edge off, a passy would be so much healthier than a drink or a smoke. Just think, this new trend could have the potential to ultimately wipe out harmful addictions as we know them!

Oh, there is that one tiny problem the experts keep bringing up. Extended passy usage could mean we'd all wind up with teeth like Austin Powers.

So it's time to give it up, babies!

TARDY TOOTH FAIRY PAYS THE PRICE

I totaled the tooth fairy. A magical childhood fantasy handed down for trillions of generations, and I wasted her faster than a roomful of know-it-all second graders. You might say I shattered the illusion tooth by tooth.

When our second child, Lauren, reached the tooth-losing age, teeth popped out quicker than the Pop-Tarts in our toaster. Lauren never waited for her teeth to get to that dangling-by-a-thread stage. As soon as one seemed the least bit wobbly, she yanked it out.

"Look, mom, another tooth!"

"Great, Lauren." I sighed. "But if you were more patient, you wouldn't need to use daddy's wrench."

Of course, I didn't entirely disapprove; she may be destined for a career in dentistry.

The nightly bedtime routine is exhausting enough, and the tooth fairy, times two kids, only prolongs the process:

"So how does the tooth fairy get here?" my daughter asks.

"Um (yawn), tooth fairy? Get here? By train." I explain.

"Train? But I thought she could fly?"

"Oh yeah, right (yawn), she can. But every other month, she gets her wings clipped and she has to come by train."

"What does she look like?"

"Oh, I never actually saw her."

"But I thought you told me she wore a glittering blue dress."

"I did?" That's right (yawn), a blue dress. Well, she doesn't wear blue every day; unlike your Mommy, she has an extensive wardrobe. Now, you better get to sleep or she won't come."

The next morning at five sharp, Lauren stomped into the bedroom and shouted into my exposed ear. "She didn't come!"

"Who didn't come?"

"The tooth fairy!"

Guilt jolted me awake. "Really? Gosh, that train must've been delayed. Uh . . . or the tooth-fairy engineers staged a strike. Yeah, that was it."

"MOM," Lauren insisted, "tell me the truth."

"Okay, okay. You see, it's just that she had too many teeth to pick up and her assistant fairy had the night off."

With each tooth, my husband and I became more forgetful and the concocted stories, more unbelievable.

"Uh . . . she was auditioning for a part in the new Disney movie and . . . no, wait a minute, Tinkerbell had a headache and she had to fill in at the castle this week."

Every parent forgets once, maybe twice, but three nights in a row? Well, the kids begin to lose their faith in fairies.

My son finally created a giant billboard, which he attached to his headboard with a large arrow pointing toward his pillow saying, "TOOTH HERE!!"

And the next night, she forgot again!

Imagining the years of therapy our son would now need, the fairy finally gave him $5 and a note of apology. He was the hit of the second grade.

"You got how much?!" His friends gasped.

"Gee, the tooth fairy never gave me more than fifty cents."

"But was she ever late?" my son asked his awe-struck peers.

"Never."

"Too bad," Marcus said shaking his head. "The later the better. The interest adds up."

Maybe I haven't single-handedly destroyed a childhood fantasy. I've just increased her value. And for this, I sincerely apologize to all the tooth fairies who managed to get it right the first night.

FORGET PQ, TRY DQ

As a regular columnist, I'm featured in the newspaper every week, but I'm certain it would be best if I didn't actually read the paper. I mean, newspapers are, like, so full of news. There's oodles of information that could lead to, dare I say it, thinking! And from there, well, you could be spurred into action, which usually results in my having to get off the couch.

Take for instance Qs. In my ignorance, Q was nothing more than the seventeenth letter in the alphabet. But after reading a few thousand newsworthy items, I've learned about the IQ (Intelligence Quotient) and EQ (Emotional Quotient) and every way in which to increase these Qs to ensure my children's maximum well-being and success.

Then, after reading a recent newspaper article, I've learned that now I should be concerned about their PQs! It seems if you really want your kid to succeed in school, you must increase their Play Quotient.

This is the latest news from Dr. Toy herself, Dr. Stevanne Auerbach, author of *Dr. Toy's Smart Play: How to Raise a Child with a High PQ*.

Sure, you're thinking, "No problem, my kids play all the time." But there's one ingredient you may have overlooked. According to Dr. Toy, PQ includes Y-O-U!

Whatever happened to the good old days when pioneer parents simply shoved a corncob doll into their child's hands, pushed them out the cabin door, and said, "Go play!"?

And they did. Unless, of course, they were hungry. Then they shucked the doll and ate it. I myself am an adult child of a PQ-less family. My parents never played with me. They shoved Tina Tears-N-Tinkle into my hands, pushed me out the front door, and said, "Go play!"

And I did! And look at me. Better yet, don't look at me. Look at my sister. She came out okay.

What Dr. Toy emphasizes is parental involvement. She says, "Get on the floor with them!"

My four year old drags out her pink plastic dollhouse with the plastic figures and gives me that look. Jenna pours the CQ (Cute Quotient) on thick. Dripping sugar, she asks, "You wanna play dolls with me, Mom?"

(Oh, no! Not dolls! Anything but dolls!) But now that I know about PQ, I have to say, "Shh . . . (cry), shh . . . (stamp feet), (pout) sure!"

My daughter is in her happy place. She's playing with her two best toys: dolly and Mommy. And I'm in my coma place. Somebody help me.

Jenna shoves a plastic doll into my hands. "You're Elizabeth," she says. "And I'm the mom and this is your baby sister."

We sit there in silence.

Then Jenna says, "Uh-oh, the baby's crying. She needs to eat. Would you put the baby in her highchair, Elizabeth? Elizabeth, I'm talking to you!"

Mustering some interest, I say, "Elizabeth, listen to your mother."

"You *are* Elizabeth," Jenna reminds me. I toss the baby in the highchair. After the baby eats, we take the baby for a walk in the stroller. We come home. We eat. We watch television. . . .

Help me! Please! I'm slipping deeper, deeper . . .

"Elizabeth would you make some popcorn? Elizabeth, get your big head out of the living room! You're crushing the dolls!"

"Huh?" I muster.

Jenna is imitating life. It's my life in a dollhouse and it's about as exciting as watching cheese mold. Oh, sure, we did get to fly off the roof a couple of times, but unfortunately, it didn't kill us.

"Uh, mom, I'm going to take a nap," I say.

"You can't take a nap," Jenna informs me. "You're a kid. You never say that," she laughs.

Lids closing. Mayday! Mayday!

Ring. Ring.

"It's the phone, Jenna! Isn't that great? It's probably someone important. . . . Hello? You're looking for a Dottie? No, there's no one here by that—wait a minute, did you say Dottie? Are you sure

you didn't say Deb? Deb, Dottie, they're so similar. I could probably help you out as well as Dottie could. Please don't hang up!"

I trudged back just in time to help Jenna grocery shop. We did
get to take the Barbie jeep, but we had to drive the speed limit.

That's it. I can't take it any longer! PQ or no PQ, I'm utilizing
my DQ, right now!

"Hey, Jenna, you want to go to Dairy Queen?"

"Yeah!"

I'm certain I'll need a double-dip cone to completely revive me.

READING UNLOCKS MANY DOORS

It was our regular reading time, that winding-down half-hour
before bed, when my children and I snuggle together on the
couch to listen to the sounds of letters and words, sentences and
phrases strung together into song.

We eagerly anticipated another melodic story sweeping us
away to foreign lands and exotic places. But tonight's tale was
choppy at best. There were obvious breaks in the rhythm, as the
novice stumbled over keys and halted on unfamiliar notes.

My son, Marcus, grew impatient. But for me, the reading
sounded as eloquent and lyrical as a Brahms' lullaby. Not for the
most skillful orator would I have turned a deaf ear to this bud-
ding newcomer. I sat on the edge of my seat in awe as the sayer
of the song deciphered and attempted the strange, new sounds.

"Look h-h-er . . . h-eer. Look. Look. Look. In, no, It . . . i-i-s
s-omething . . . dah, dah . . . NO, it's bah, bah big. It is something BIG!"

"Bravo!" I cried. "You're READING, Lauren! You're reading
all by yourself."

My daughter's smile grew wider with the realization.
Consonant by consonant, street sign by store sign, cereal box by
ketchup bottle, the mystery behind the locked door had creaked
open.

Of all the landmarks in my children's young lives, none has
astounded me more than watching them learn to read. Like
learning to walk, it was a gradual process, which began with a
crawl and moved to a coffee table.

Lauren would sit on the couch with an upside-down Dr. Seuss book talking animatedly to the pages. She'd scribble lines on paper and say, "What did I write, mom? Can you read it?"

"It's wonderful," I'd say, "and one day, all those lines will make letters and words."

"When, mom?" she'd ask with a longing in her voice.

"Soon," I told her. "Soon."

No expensive phonics tapes speeded or impeded the process, just mom and dad reading the rhymes of Mother Goose and Dr. Seuss. We followed the adventures of the Boxcar Children and Curious George and solved mysteries with Cam Jansen and Nate the Great. We sang the famous "ABC" song on car trips and played the "A Is for Apple; B Is for Baseball" game, with each child taking a turn at sounding out the beginning letter of the word.

Once they became familiar with the first sounds, I introduced my children to their first word. That magical first word was C-A-T. And because they were accustomed to rhyming, I simply changed the first letter, and soon, they could read R-A-T, S-A-T, H-A-T, and P-A-T.

My daughter pointed to me and said "F-A-T." So I quickly moved onto D-O-G and L-O-G and F-R-O-G and H-O-G.

With all the pieces in place, my children were still unable to nudge open the door until they possessed one more skill: an innate ability that kicks in at different ages and stages for each child, as unexplainable as the rules of reading itself. But when it's there, your child will tell you.

Now that Lauren has mastered and accepted the inconsistencies of c for cat and k for kite and the silent e in make, the ph in phone sounds like f, and she believes she can do just about anything.

Another grown-up mystery has been revealed. She can interpret her world and take marvelous journeys without me now. While curled up on the couch, under the shade of a swaying willow, or beneath the bed covers with a flashlight, Lauren will fly into outer space, traipse through the Amazon on a safari, and meet Tom Sawyer, Jo March, and Laura Ingalls Wilder in the big woods.

Each new adventure will expand and enrich her life. Like her brother before her, she will soon inform me of places and people I know nothing about and be shocked by my limited knowledge.

The next night, as we sit down to read, Lauren hands me the book and lays her head on my shoulder.

"Read to me, Mom," she says.

"But why?" I ask, puzzled by her request. "You can read by yourself now."

"Because," she says snuggling closer, "I like the way you sound."

CHAPTER 2

Toils with Tikes, Yikes!

Parents are the bones on which children cut their teeth.
—Peter Ustinov

FAMILY MEETINGS: A LESSON IN DEMOCRACY?

I recently read a book favoring family meetings. The author wrote that regular meetings could provide an opportunity for families to set down rules, solve problems, and create a close-knit bond. So, in an effort to get my busy family on the same page, or at least reading the same book, I suggested we try one.

Our first meeting began with a huge bowl of buttered popcorn—and a large wooden spoon that served as the gavel. The popcorn kept the more reluctant members, like my husband, at the table. The gavel kept members swatting at each other, until we passed our first family rule: "No gavel whacking during meetings."

It didn't take long for my husband and I to realize that we loved family meetings. After a few years in the work force and after attending hundreds of meetings, we were at a distinct advantage. The only difference was that at work we weren't the bosses, but at home, well, I got to be Judge Judy!

I set down rules. There was to be no television during the school week, homework must commence after one hour of playtime, and chores were to be completed every Saturday morning.

My husband set down rules. Interrupting a family member when he or she is talking on the phone results in a time-out, name-calling requires the guilty party to write the other person's proper name twenty times, and yelling at another family member calls for a heartfelt apology.

Once we were satisfied that our children had enough rules to keep them busy until they moved out, we asked if they had any problems or suggestions. Naturally, they were too stunned to talk. So we quickly typed up the minutes and had each member sign on the bottom line.

Our second family meeting was more of the same. It wasn't until the third family meeting that we began to lose control. Ultimately, we blame the school system. Our son started studying the branches of government, and then those teachers had to go and explain the difference between a democracy and a dictatorship.

"Excuse me," Marcus interrupted. "But I think it's only fair that Lauren and I talk first this time."

Sensing mutiny, my husband and I shouted, "No!"

"Apologize!" Marcus demanded.

"WHAT?!" we gasped.

"Rule number fifteen," Lauren explained. "You owe us an apology."

"We're SORRY," I said in exasperation.

"I don't thing that was heartfelt, Mom." Marcus indicated.

"Okay, we're truly sorry for yelling," my husband said. "And yes, you can talk first."

Marcus pulled a long list from his pocket. "First, we have a problem with chores."

"Chores are a rule," I smugly reminded him.

"Oh, we're not complaining about the chores," said Lauren. "It's the payment plan."

"Payment plan?"

"Yeah," said Marcus. "We do the chores, but you always forget to give us our allowances. By my calculations, you owe us $20 a piece. And we'd like to make a new rule. If you don't pay us an allowance, you and dad must do our chores the following week."

"Sounds fair to me," added Lauren.

It was at that moment I discovered the distinct flaw in family meetings: fairness. The book suggested that children be included as full participants and parents must listen deeply and value their ideas. The book obviously needed a rewrite.

"Now, it's my turn," Lauren piped up. "I'd like a hamster."

"A WHAT? NO WAY, LADY! NO RODENT IS STEPPING FOOT INTO MY HOUSE."

"Careful, mom. You'll have to stop interrupting or be removed from the meeting. Rule twenty-five," said Marcus. "Go ahead, Lauren."

"Thank you, dear brother. I checked out some books at the library about hamsters and wrote down all the things I need to do."

"You did this?" my husband gasped, as he poured over her pages of extensive research. "Wow, I'm impressed."

"Don't be impressed," I nudged my husband.

"We can't ignore her request," my husband whispered back.

"Yes, we can!" I cried.

"Mom, would you stop interrupting," Marcus cautioned.

Lauren continued. "I'd like everyone to read my notes and bring back your thoughts on hamsters to the next family meeting."

"You bet I'll bring my thoughts, and they won't be PRETTY!" I shouted.

"Mom, I'm sorry," Marcus announced. "We've warned you enough times. You've been ousted from this meeting."

"Wait a minute," I cried. "You can't do this! The family meetings were my idea. And I vote to abolish them, immediately. Honey help!" I begged, glancing at my husband.

He just sat there. Obviously, he was too stunned to talk.

Family meetings—just another opportunity for parents to realize who really rules the roost.

SHRUNKEN-NOODLE SYNDROME

I appreciate a good educational game as much as the next parent does. So, while zipping through the empty-your-wallet-on-us toy store, the Brainquest board game caught my eye.

"It's okay to be smart!" the box proclaimed.

"Now, see this," I said to my children. "THIS is a great game. It's fun and educational, much better than those video games you drool over. And we're all going to play it tonight. . . . Kids? Kids? Where are you hiding? Yup, just as soon as the security guards track you down, we're buying this game."

Later that evening, the entire family sat down to play. I couldn't wait to move my plastic playing piece shaped like a question mark onto the little red schoolhouse labeled Start. My husband couldn't wait till the game was over.

The object of the game was to roll the die and answer the trivia question pertaining to your grade level in school. If you answered correctly, you moved your question marker. The first marker to reach the square marked Finish was the winner.

"You have to answer all the sixth-grade questions and subtract two numbers from the die, because you finished junior high, Mom and Dad," my fifth grader, Lauren, pointed out.

"No problem!" I said, throwing the die. "You're talking to a straight-A student here." (Well, almost, except for that C in math, but that was Mrs. Malvin's fault for giving us all those fractions.)

"True or false? All rivers east of the Continental Divide flow in an easterly direction."

"The Continental? I think that was a line dance in the '40s? I'll say false."

"True," my sixth grader, Marcus, corrected me. "Dad's turn. Can you find a saguaro in a desert, in a forest, or in a jungle?"

"Saguaro? Isn't that a new minivan?" my husband asked, scratching his head.

"Desert," Lauren piped up. "That's a cactus," she explained, moving her dad's marker back to Start, which is where he happened to be anyway.

My kids effortlessly answered questions in their grade levels, and even two grades higher, for more bonus points. Their plastic pieces whipped around the board, leaving my question marker questioning why it ever wanted to play this dumb game in the first place!

Because now, my kids knew the truth . . . the truth they may have surmised when I forgot to make brownies for school or when their father frantically searched for the eyeglasses perched atop his head. The evidence they gleaned when I absent-mindedly left their baby sister in the cart at Wal-Mart!

Our parental brains were shrinking!

Yes, we parents are all victims of the Shrunken-Noodle Syndrome. Ha! You laugh—denial—just another shrinkage side effect.

According to a recent University of Pennsylvania study, men between the ages of eighteen and forty-five lose brain tissue in their frontal lobes. This tissue loss "curbs memory, concentration, and reasoning power." Professor Gur (unfortunately, he can only remember the first syllable of his last name) said shrinking brains may make men grumpier, too.

Frontal-lobe loss explains how it's possible for your husband to watch the kids an entire afternoon and forget to feed them lunch. And you thought he was too busy watching the sports channel.

But women aren't immune to the Shrunken-Noodle Syndrome. A team of British scientists discovered that pregnant women suffer from brain shrinkage and may not regain their full mental powers until six months after giving birth! The shrinking results in memory loss and absent-mindedness. However, since some of the scientists on the team were men with shrinking brains, the studies are somewhat inconclusive.

I have my own theory. At night, our already puny brains must suddenly reduce to the size of peas. I know this because when our baby, Jenna, would cry, my husband would nudge me out of a sound sleep and say, "It's your turn to get up, Deb."

And I'd say, "I rocked her the last hour. It's your turn."

And he'd say, "Have you lost your mind?! I rocked her last!"

And I'd say, "Listen, you brainless boob! I rocked her last! It's your turn!"

"IS not!"

"IS too!"

This brainless blabbering continues until big-brained Jenna

climbs out of her crib, crawls into our bed, and breaks up the fight.

Now, thanks to Brainquest, Jenna's not the only family member clued into our pea brains.

"Marcus, it's time to play piano," I remind my son.

"But I already played piano today, Mom. Don't you remember? You helped me with the more specific new chords."

"That was today?" I ask.

"Of course, it was today. Don't you remember?" Marcus says shaking his big-brained head. He pats my arm and steers me toward the couch. "Why don't you lay your little head down, Mom."

"Dad, can we have our allowance?" Our daughter, Lauren, asks.

"But I thought I just paid you your allowance yesterday." He says, scratching his teeny-tiny forehead.

"That was last week, dad. Don't you remember?"

"Of course, I remember. Here's your allowance."

"Uh, Dad, did you forget?"

"Forget what?"

"You gave us a raise."

FAMILY PORTRAITS PORTRAY THE TRUTH

If you've ever given serious thought to auditioning for the next *Survivor* episode, there's only one skill capable of making you tough enough, not only to compete, but to win: take a family portrait.

To create a pictorial directory, our church was offering parishioners a photo session.

"Let's do this," my husband encouraged. "We get a free 8 x 10."

"Ha, ha!" I laughed, holding onto his shoulder for support. "You think a free photo is going to make up for the suffering, the tears, and the posttraumatic stress that comes with taking a family portrait?"

My naïve husband, who had been conveniently at work for the last fifteen years of Christmas photos, replied, "What's so difficult? We find coordinating outfits, we take the picture, and we walk out with a free family photo."

"Ah ha! Ah ha! Ah ha ha ha!" I laughed, doubling over.

"Okay, get up off the floor, Deb, and breath into this paper bag."

The day of the photo session, our son appeared in his favorite skateboard T-shirt.

"You can't wear that!" my husband snapped. "The words 'ghetto child' might be a bit DISTRACTING!"

The middle daughter shuffled by in her big, washed-out jeans.

"March right upstairs and put on the outfit I laid out on your bed," my husband said through clenched teeth.

The kindergartner twirled into view in her favorite pink dress.

"Honey," my husband said gently, "pink is going to clash with the red we're all supposed to wear."

"But pink is my favorite color!" she blubbered, flinging herself onto the floor in a heap of despair.

For the next few hours, our house was filled with yipping, crying, and whimpering, and that was just from the dog. By then, the neighborhood-watch group had called the police and an officer was ringing our doorbell.

He took one look at our various stages of dress and undress and said, "We took our photo last week. Good luck," then ran down the front steps.

Finally, everyone was dressed in something acceptable, although coordinating was definitely a debatable term. We arrived at our scheduled appointment a half-hour early.

"Please take us now!" my husband begged.

The woman had seen that look before and rushed us into the makeshift studio. Thanks to the invention of the computer, every family can view their photo on a nearby monitor before it's printed.

Flash!

Son's eyes closed.

Flash!

Daughter glaring at father.

Flash!

Kindergartner draping pink shawl over her red-and-khaki outfit.

Flash!

Father crying.

Flash!

Mother breathing into a paper bag.

After about twenty takes, we finally had a decent shot. Then, the picky photographer pointed out a petty flaw.

"Your daughter is picking her nose."

My husband said, "Print it."

Yes, another family portrait complete and soon ready to take its place of honor in the bottom of the box in the back of the closet, marked Photos.

EVERYBODY GROWS UP AT CAMP

"What do you mean I wasn't there when you learned to ride your bike?!" I balked at my he-has-one-more-SpaghettiO-than-me middle child. "I was the one who taught you," I reminded her.

"Not really," my preteen clarified. "The day I rode by myself, you were in the house watching a soap opera."

In an effort to defend myself, I asked, "What about the 6,000 days before that split second, when I held on to the back of your bike seat, huffing and puffing my way around the block?"

"Yeah, but," she said, discounting those memories with a pop of her tutti-frutti bubblegum, "the day I actually learned, your soap opera was more important. You didn't even come outside to watch me."

"You're WRONG, Lauren!" I barked, dismissing her version with a flick of my kitchen towel.

"Besides," I thought to myself, "even if she was right, it probably occurred on the same day that Luke and Laura married for the tenth time. Who could blame a mother for not wanting to miss that history-making moment?"

Unfortunately, I didn't have time to pout about it. I was too busy preparing the ungrateful child for a week away at Camp-Cost-a-Lot, guaranteed to provide your kid with memories they would selectively forget for a lifetime.

I individually wrapped all of her prettiest outfits, the ones that set off her blue eyes, in tissue paper before carefully laying them in her suitcase.

"Gee, mom, I'm going to camp, not the Holiday Inn," Lauren said while smashing her favorite pillow on top of the pile."

Yes, camp week couldn't come soon enough for both of us.

The moment finally arrived. We left Lauren in the hands of two counselors who sat perched atop the cabin bureau like Buddhas, only without the bellies, imparting vast experiences of camping wisdom to their awe-struck followers sitting on the floor below. I stared into the fresh, young faces of the girls who would take care of my baby for a week.

"It looks like it was just yesterday that they learned to feed themselves," I whispered to my husband.

"Just think," he reminded me, "for an entire six days, we won't have to hear about who has more marshmallows in their breakfast cereal bowl."

I bent down to kiss my daughter. "Don't forget to wear sunscreen."

The week without Lauren was quieter. But it didn't take more than a day before the quiet became deafening. Although I had filled her suitcase with a note to read every day—short little notes like "Remember to flash that awesome smile," "Have a great day," and the one from her brother that read, "Don't fart while sitting on the horse or he might pass out"—I decided to sit down and write her a letter. But what I wrote surprised even me:

Dear Lauren, remember when you told me I was watching a soap opera the day you learned to ride your bike? At first, I was mad and didn't want to believe that it was true. But if that's how you remember it, then it is true. And I want to tell you how sorry I am for not rushing out to watch you. I am very proud of you and all your accomplishments and I will be watching more closely from now on!

I wrote other letters after that. Her brother wrote letters. Grandma wrote letters. Even Champ, the dog, sent a paw print. The only one who didn't send any letters was Lauren!

But it didn't matter. Camp had already given me what I needed most. In the quiet spaces, I learned to let go of the mother-is-always-right mindset and gave my daughter back her truth.

Saturday, after a loving reunion, which was just like a scene in *From Here to Eternity*—or maybe it was "Joanie Loves Chachi"—

as she ran into my open arms and even nodded to her brother, I unzipped her suitcase to begin sorting the laundry. There at the bottom of her dirty clothes was a crumpled letter signed and ready to be mailed to the DiSandro family. I opened it.

The shaky penmanship brought tears to my eyes. It wasn't the short paragraphs filled with her daily camp activities, but the P.S.—not the first P.S. that she wrote to her brother, saying, "Marcus, you are a disgusting pig," but the second P.S. she wrote to me—which said, "Mom, it's okay. Maybe I was wrong about the bike thing. Love, Lauren."

LOVE IS IN THE LAUNDRY

"Mom, what's the difference between infatuation and love?"

"Sixty loads of laundry," I grumbled while separating the whites from the mud stained.

"Really, Mom. I need to know," my son insisted.

"Listen, Marcus," I replied. "If asking me some silly question is your latest technique for getting out of homework, you can forget it. I'm on to you."

"But this *is* my homework," Marcus assured me. "It's for my sex-education class."

"For your what class?!! How come I didn't know about this class?" I asked, attempting to cover my underwear pile with a towel.

"You signed the permission slip," he reminded me.

"I thought you wanted to take sax lessons!"

"Well, I'm supposed to ask my parents this question for homework."

"Isn't your father home yet?" I asked hopefully.

"Nope. When I called him at work, he said to ask you the question. Oh, and he said to tell you he'd be late tonight."

"No kidding."

"So what is it?" Marcus pressed.

"What's what?"

"The difference between infatuation and love?"

"Let's see." I said, stalling for time and some kind of revelation. "Well, um, infatuation has to do with how you look. If you think someone is really good looking and that's all you care about, you're infatuated."

My son looked confused. "Are you saying that to be in love you have to think the other person looks ugly?"

"No, that's not what I meant. Forget that. Infatuation is when . . . uh, when you . . . well, when you think you're in love, but you're really not."

"Huh?"

"Okay, let's try again. Infatuation happens fast. Let's say, you see a girl in sixth-period math, and you like the way she twirls her hair around her pencil, and by seventh-period English, you think you're in love, but you're really just infatuated."

"Courtney Fishburn."

"Who?"

"Courtney Fishburn twirls her hair around her pencil."

"See!" I said encouragingly.

"But I'm not infatuated with her."

"Well, you have to like the way she twirls her hair around her pencil."

"I do, but I'm still not infatuated with her."

"Okay," I said wiping the sweat off my brow with a dirty bath towel and tossing it into the washing machine. "Let's forget about infatuation for a minute. We'll talk about love. Now, love goes deeper than infatuation. In the classic movie, *Love Story*, with Ryan O'Neal and Ali McGraw, this guy was being a real jerk to his sick wife. It took him, like, the whole movie to figure it out, because guys don't usually realize when they're acting like jerks. . . .'"

"MOM!"

". . . So he goes to his wife to apologize and she interrupts him and says, 'Love means never having to say you're sorry.' It was so romantic (sniff, sniff). Everybody in the audience was crying (sob, sob)."

"Mom," Marcus said while tossing me a dirty T-shirt, "are you saying that when you're infatuated, you have to say you're sorry, but when you're in love, you don't?"

"No! That's not what I'm saying at all," I gasped while dabbing at my eyes with the corner of the T-shirt. "Come to think of it, that was the stupidest line in the whole movie! Wow, it's amazing how your entire outlook on love changes after sixteen years of marriage, and reading Dr. Laura's *Ten Stupid Things Women Do to Mess up Their Lives*."

"Mom, I can't write all that!" my son said in irritation.

"Wait, I think I've got it," I said enthusiastically. "Infatuation is the way I look at Tom Cruise."

"Like when you get all dreamy eyed and start drooling on the couch?"

"And love," I said, ignoring him, "is the way I look at your father."

"Like when he leaves his dirty underwear on the floor?"

"Sort of, but it's also the way I look when your dad remembers to pick up milk on the way home from work. That's love. When he takes my car in to be serviced before I take it on a trip, that's love. When I cook dinner even though I don't feel like it, that's love. Compromise, commitment, and forgiveness are love. And trying to get this mustard off your dad's dress shirt is driving me crazy, but I do it because I love him! Okay?!"

"Okay, mom. I think I get it."

"Good."

"Oh, and for right now, I'll take infatuation over love. It may be disgusting, but it's a lot less work."

"Marcus, I think you've got it."

OPEN YOUR WALLET WIDE AND SAY AAAHHH!

There comes a time in every parent's life when you realize exactly what motivates you to get up and drag your ever-expanding fanny to work every morning: orthodontia. Translation: "Open your wallet wide and say AAAHHH!"

My husband and I recently discovered this phenomenon when our dentist said we had to. Until this significant and painful moment, we had lived in a save-your-pennies-for-a-rainy-day delusion.

It seemed everyone knew our son needed thousand-dollar rubber bands before we did. On the day he was born, my mother took one look at him and said, "He's beautiful and he's going to need braces."

When he smiled his first drool-filled grin, the baby photographer flashed the bulb and said, "I'll do his twelve-year photo for free."

"Great. Is that some kind of special promotion?" I asked.

"No. I always give parents whose kids wear braces a freebie." After Marcus smiled again, he added, "Okay, I'll make that two free photos."

I had to admit that I noticed my son's teeth popping out at obtuse angles and curves only found in high-school geometry books, but I kept saying, "They'll straighten out when his other teeth come in."

I didn't even know what orthodontia was. I came from a family of straight choppers. My own teeth were perfectly spaced as a child, except for the front two, which sported a gap wide enough to push through an entire Ho Ho. Picture David Letterman in pigtails.

I was an instant hit at birthday parties. Dubbed as the one-and-only human fountain, I sprayed a steam of water through that gap in a perfect arch. When they turned the colored patio lights on me, Old Faithful was a drip in comparison.

Then, at the mature age of twenty-five, the dentist added a little bonding cement and my famous gap became a distant, although pleasant, memory. Had I realized the enormous number of cocktail parties I would no longer be invited to, I might've reconsidered!

Last month at the bank, the teller merely glanced at my son and asked, "Would you be interested in our new loan program?"

I knew what she was getting at, and frankly, I'd had enough. I leaned over the counter and yelled, "Look, lady, my kid does not need braces, and even if he did, I certainly wouldn't need a loan to pay for them!"

All the other parents, furiously filling out loan applications, broke into peels of laughter.

One lady commented, "You are so funny. Have you ever considered stand-up comedy?"

"Why, yes, I have," I replied. "But what's the joke?"

I soon found out when I walked into the orthodontist's office. Before proceeding beyond the entryway, the receptionist instructed me to lay my purse on an x-ray machine, which immediately detected the denomination of all the bills inside my wallet.

Then the orthodontist greeted us with the whitest, straightest smile this side of Jim Carrey. His office could have been featured in *House Beautiful*. I wanted to live there. Plush couches, tasteful wallpaper, video games, soft music—all the comforts that oral adjustments can buy.

Mr. *House Beautiful* took one look at Marcus and said, "Mrs. DiSandro, your son does not need braces."

"He what?! That's wonderful!" I cried, kissing Smiley on the cheek and dancing out of the office.

He pulled me back by my purse strap. "What Marcus needs is an expansion appliance, an appliance that I will cement to the roof of his mouth. You will be given a key, and three times a day, every day for the next few months, you must turn the key without fail. Do you understand?"

I stood there with my mouth hanging open so wide I will most likely need a contraction appliance to close it. Finally, I gulped in enough air to ask, "What happens when I turn the key?"

"Every time you turn the key, the price of the appliance automatically expands."

I let out a whoop of laughter and patted the doctor on the back. "Oh, that's so funny, Doc. Have you ever considered stand-up comedy?"

"Yes," he replied. "Yes, I have. But what's the joke?"

"Never mind, Doc, just hurry up. I've got to get to the bank before it closes."

COMMUNITY SERVICE COMFORTS THE NEEDY

It would've been so much easier to let him go by himself. But I knew he needed me, although he gave that typical preteen shrug and mumbled, "Whatever."

Marcus's religious-education class had volunteered to help the residents at a nearby retirement home with their bingo game. So, on a sunny Saturday afternoon, my son and I found ourselves in a place where wheelchairs and walkers were as common as a middle school full of baggy pants.

Bingo was to start at 2 P.M. I could just imagine what some of the seniors were thinking as they hobbled, or rolled, over to the tables and waited for one of the eager youngsters to bring them their bingo cards: "Oh, great, here come those kids fulfilling their community-service hours. I just hope they don't pull out my IV again, step on my sore foot, or worse yet, cheat me at bingo. I swore the last time they were here I had bingo. But that perky girl scout said it was B6, not G66. These young whippersnappers think they know everything."

Of course, many of the residents said exactly what was on their minds:

"What are the prizes?" a woman barked.

"Gee, I don't know." I replied.

"If we're playing for a lousy piece of fruit, I'm not playing!" she pouted.

"I'm sure it'll be something better than . . . oh, gee, look at the size of those bananas," I finished, as a cartful of fruit was rolled to the front of the room.

"Told ya," she grunted. "I'm only playing one game."

As the game began, my son helped the woman with her bingo markers. I kept an eye on the other two ladies at the table. One was quite capable of filling her own card. The other seemed less interested, so I helped her. Frankly, I was in a quiet panic. I worried that she might actually win. And then what was I supposed to do? Wake her up? Maybe I could just raise her arm and wave it gently, without disturbing her slumber. But I didn't know the bingo policy here. Maybe a sleeping player wasn't allowed to win, and the other players would suddenly start throwing fruit at me and use their canes as spears.

As I stood sweating, a new gentleman arrived and was wheeled to a nearby table. I quickly abandoned my snoozing senior and set him up with bingo cards.

"Are we playing for fruit, again?" he asked.

"Uh, well, yeah." I said.

"WHAT?!!"

"Yes," I admitted.

"WHAT?!!"

Finally, noticing the hearing aid in his ear, I shouted at the top of my lungs, "YES!"

"You don't have to shout. I can hear you."

"We have a bingo!" the caller announced.

I looked around. Everybody was staring at our table.

"Oh, no, we don't have a bingo. I was just telling him we were playing for fruit."

"WHAT?!" the senior asked again.

"No bingo!" I shouted.

"We're not playing anymore?" he asked.

"YES! I MEAN, NO! I MEAN, WE'RE STILL PLAYING!"

The game finally resumed and my senior wound up winning two pieces of fruit. I congratulated him on his victory and gladly went to sit with the other parent volunteers. A group of Girl Scouts were up next (no wonder these seniors were so exhausted) and our services were no longer needed. I watched my son talking with the senior at his table. He seemed somewhat at ease and interested in what the woman had to say. Later, when I went to collect him, the woman turned to me and said, "Your son is a nice young man. He reminds me of my grandson."

"Thank you," I replied, touching her hand. I looked down. Her arthritic fingers reminded me of my father's. Instead of pulling away, I wanted to rub them against my cheek.

It was three o'clock. My son's hour of community service was fulfilled. We walked outside deep in our own thoughts. It was then that I realized I had not come for my son. Knowing how little I had volunteered in the various communities in which we've lived, I had come to assuage my own guilt. Oh, sure, I donate to the food pantry and clothing drives and pick a name or two off the tree at Christmas. But I'm young, healthy, and capable of doing so much more.

Playing bingo had been a minor moment, compared to the millions of volunteers willing to forgo a bit of discomfort to help the sick, the dying, the old, or the lonely. But now, I know what keeps them coming back. You walk in feeling uncomfortable; you walk out feeling comforted.

CHAPTER 3

Divides and Multiplies?

When I was fourteen, I was amazed at how unintelligent my father was. By the time I turned twenty-one, I was astounded how much he had learned in the last seven years.

—Mark Twain

CLASS HELPER FLUNKS OUT

The problem with volunteering at your child's school is that one day the duties you are asked to perform may far exceed your academic capabilities. Being a college graduate, I didn't expect that time to come until, oh, about . . . sixth or seventh grade. So when Marcus was in fourth grade and asked me to help out in his class, I assumed my skill level might not only be sufficient, but also quite possibly superior to at least half of the students in his class. A few weeks prior to Marcus's invite, in my daughter's first-grade class, I had spent the afternoon cutting shapes from colored construction paper and writing names on glitter-studded choo-choo trains. I assumed fourth grade would be more of the same, only with slightly more sophisticated choo-choos.

"You can sit over here," Marcus's teacher said, leading me to a miniature desk of my own right outside the classroom door.

"What did I do wrong?" I asked. "How come I can't sit in there with all the other kids?"

"This is where the volunteer parents work," she explained.

"Oh, sure, no problem." I replied with a chuckle. "It's just that when I went to school, the bad kids had to sit outside the class-room. And I'm not a bad kid! Am I?"

"No, of course not, Mrs. DiSandro. You're doing just fine," she assured me.

Thirty seconds later, she steered a student into the seat next to mine. "You sit here until you can behave yourself, young man!"

I smiled sympathetically. The projects were simple enough at first: thirty copies of this math assignment, six collated copies of this work sheet, etc.

My son would sneak out periodically to monitor my progress. Feeling proud of his mother's volunteering accomplishments, he'd whisper to his friends, "That's my mom. She makes the best copies."

Marcus's teacher soon returned with another pile of papers. "I'd like you to fill out these answer keys for me."

"Answer keys, sure. Uh . . . no prob . . . wait a minute, where are the answers to the answer key?" I asked with a note of panic in my voice.

Marcus's teacher laughed. In fact, I think she even cackled. "There are no answers until you fill in the blanks."

"ME?! But this is math!" I gulped. "And—oh, my gosh!" I cried, examining the paper more closely. "These are story prob-lems!"

"Yes, they are. Don't you just love them?" she oozed.

"No, I don't love them. They bring back nightmares. Listen, I came here to cut out shapes and stuff. Don't you have any choo-choos for me to decorate?"

"Oh, Marcus," she cackled again, while slinking back into the classroom, "your mother has such a wit."

The first answer key was titled "Smart Shopping." It read: "Save money by looking for bargains and figure out which ad offers the lower price."

I breathed a sigh of relief. With three kids, grocery shopping was my life.

The first ad read: "Eggplant on a stick only four for $2.80."
The second ad read: "Eggplant on a stick only three for $1.95."

Thank goodness. The first question was a cinch. My answer read: "The smart shopper would not buy any eggplant on a stick, because no one in the family would eat it!"

The next math problem was about a family vacation. The family left from El Paso, Texas, on Wednesday and then spent the entire week traveling all over Dallas and Houston. I was supposed to keep track of the mileage and determine the number on the odometer when the family returned home on Friday.

Well, I couldn't help wondering why the family would decide to return on Friday, in the midst of rush-hour traffic. This really bugged me and I figured it was probably a trick question. Teachers loved giving trick questions when I was in school. Then it suddenly occurred to me that the kids in the car were probably acting up and fighting, so the parents decided to return early. During the scuffle, one of the kids toppled into the front seat and accidentally knocked the odometer back to zero. So the answer would be zero. As I was writing my answer, I felt someone peering over my shoulder.

"That's not the right answer!" my son gasped. "You're wrong, Mom!" he exclaimed, backing away from me, his eyes filled with shock and disappointment.

"Wait!" I called to him, realizing the seriousness of the moment—that moment when your child suddenly discovers you're not the all-knowing creature he once believed you to be. I chose my words carefully. "Marcus," I whispered, "if you fill out this answer key for me, I promise to make your bed for a week!"

"Cool!" He said, grabbing the paper.

"Not so fast, Marcus."

Busted! Marcus's teacher was standing right behind us.

"Mrs. DiSandro, I would like you to go to the principal's office."

"No, not the principal's office," I begged. "I still have nightmares about Mr. Burger's big wall clock with the spider hands and . . ."

"Calm down, Mrs. DiSandro, if you promise to go to the kindergarten room and cut out shapes, we can put this whole thing behind us."

"Shapes? I can do shapes. Wait a minute. These aren't geometric shapes by any chance, are they? Geometry, talk about scary!"

ORDER YOUR MUG SHOTS TODAY!

The outside of the school packet read: "If this face is special to you today, imagine how you'll feel ten years from now."

I stared down at my child's school photos peeking through the plastic window and thought: "I don't have to imagine it. I already know how I'll feel—this is one of the ugliest pictures of my kid I have ever laid eyes on!"

I immediately filled out the customer-service card that came with the photos and checked the box that read, "I think my package is incorrect," and then wrote:

"There must be some mistake. This can't possibly be the cute, photogenic kid I gave birth to! Couldn't you have combed her bangs? Couldn't you have told her to uncross her eyes? Couldn't you have removed the piece of broccoli stuck between her two front teeth?!"

In their defense, it is possible that the school photographers come straight from their day jobs—at the prison. Sometimes they must get mixed up, which may explain why my daughter was asked to hold a board with numbers across her chest.

The trouble starts the day they bring home the order form. Parents can choose from a variety of different packets, with a range of photo sizes. The packets read like your basic income-tax form: "If you'd like Packet A but want additional wallets from the special billfolds in Packet C, check Packet A minus B plus C, then add $6.00 for the special just-because-we-feel-like-it charge, and check Packet D for a wall calendar, coffee mug, and future prison shot."

When the big day finally arrives, like any conscientious mom, I always take special care to see that my children are neat, clean, and well rested. Unfortunately, this day has never coincided with picture day. The actual photo op always falls on the morning everybody oversleeps, misses the bus, rummages through the laundry basket for an I-can-wear-this-one-more-time T-shirt, and dashes out the door looking like Major Bed Head.

Recently, I discovered that my inability to remember picture day might have to do with Repressed Memory Syndrome. My brain is attempting to block out the past trauma of my own school-photo years. Unlike me, my mother never forgot picture day. The night before, she'd scrub my hair until my scalp fell off. Then she wound the squeaky strands around bobby pins and bolted them down with machine screws.

"Pains of beauty," she'd remind me. Pains of beauty? When I got my pictures back, there was no mistaking the uncanny resemblance of Don King and Phyllis Diller.

Last week, my daughter called, frantic, from school.

"Mom, it's picture day and you forgot to turn in the order form." I immediately rushed the packet to school and brought it directly to my daughter's classroom. She came to the door.

I took one look at her dirty shirt, disheveled hair, and thought, *Well, there goes $20.95 down the drain.* "Lauren," I said, preparing for the worst, "you didn't just have your picture taken, did you?"

"Of course not, Mom."

"That's a relief," I sighed, grabbing a comb from my purse.

"Our class went right after lunch."

When my son brought his photos home from middle school, I glanced through the package window and asked, "When's retake day?"

"What's wrong with it?" he asked, offended. "I showed my teeth like you told me to."

"That's great, honey," I said gently, "but I can also see your tonsils."

What choice does a parent really have? What kind of parent refuses to buy their child's school photos?

A smart one, I thought.

As I picked up the photos of my daughter to return to the school, I looked again at her smiling face. This time I saw the devilish grin that is truly my daughter's, the messy bangs that let me know she probably had a fun day on the playground. *Maybe this is what the school photos are all about,* I thought. *A true picture of your child, not some fancied-up version for photo day. Could it be possible that this was the photo worth framing after all?*

NOT! I jotted down the retake day on my calendar and called my mother.

"Mom," I said, "how do you make those pin curls?"

I'M ALL FOR SAVING THE EARTH BUT . . .

I performed stretching exercises, secured the laces on my gym shoes, ran in place to build up endurance, then flipped the light switch and made a mad dash into the kitchen pantry.

I flung canned goods on the shelf and shoved pasta and peas into every available cranny. *Hurry! Hurry!* I said to myself. Time is running out!

I still had half of a bag of groceries to go when the warning signal flashed and poof! Blackout.

"Help, help!" I shouted from the deepest, darkest depths of dry goods and nonperishables.

Suddenly, I heard a voice say, "Go toward the light."

"What light?" I snapped.

A flashlight beam appeared and I stumbled toward it.

My husband stood on the other end, shaking his head. "Must you always make restocking the pantry such a dramatic event?"

"ME?" I cried. "Since you installed that flashing, automatic shutoff switch on the light, I've had to train with the Olympic triathlon team in order to put my groceries away."

"We're saving energy, not to mention money," he reminded me.

"Just flip the switch and move out of my way," I said, running in place. "I've got to stock the creamed corn and the string beans before the next blackout."

After the exhausting stock-a-thon, I decided to reward myself with a long hot soak in the tub. As I headed toward the bathroom, I felt someone behind me and turned to face a full jury.

"You can't take a bath!" my kindergartner said. "My teacher says to save the water for the fish and take a lukewarm shower." My two older children set the stopwatch and my husband waved the water bill.

After a school semester on saving energy and learning about

the three Rs—reuse, reduce, and recycle—my children are out to save the Earth, and my husband is glowing like a light bulb, an energy-saving fluorescent one, of course. He now has a small army of allies in his mission to reduce the utility bills. He finally let go of the phone bill, realizing that some missions are impossible.

I know I don't own this land, that I'm just borrowing it from my children, but I wish the loan included a few things I've grown accustomed to—heat, for instance! Maybe it's just a petty personal thing, but during the winter months, I happen to like the temperature inside my home to be warmer than the temperature outside!

While eating dinner with some difficulty one evening, due to the thermal mittens I wore to prevent frostbite, I gingerly broached the temperature topic: "Don't you think it's a tad cold in here?" I asked as whiffs of blue smoke escaped from my blue lips.

"Not at all," my family replied.

"Then how do you explain the frosts on these green beans?" I chattered. But there was no deterring them. They were on a steady course and I was just an annoying obstacle, a piece of litter to be picked up and put in its proper receptacle.

My children routinely rummage through the kitchen garbage, removing all the recyclable items I somehow missed. They hold up each indiscretion and stare at me as if I've just sold a secret to Russia.

"This is a number two, mom. You've got to look at the bottom of these containers," my son reprimanded me.

"It's so dark in here. I couldn't read the number," I said in my defense.

"The Earth is crying!" my kindergartner explained.

"Then get her a Kleenex!" I snapped.

I was beginning to unwind. My teeth were gritty with toothpaste because I couldn't leave the water on long enough to rinse. Icicles hung from my wet hair and I hadn't worn a pair of matched socks in weeks, due to low-wattage light bulbs! I was all set to tell my family they could save the Earth, but I was moving to Mars, when my husband walked in with movie tickets.

"What's this?" I asked.

"Well, with all the money we've been saving on utility bills, I figured we could swing a baby-sitter, dinner, and a movie out tonight."

"Turn off these lights, kids!" I shouted. "And turn down the heat another two degrees. It's like a furnace in here."

COLOR MY WORLD BUT NOT MY KID!

Kindergarten has sure changed since I was a kid. Gone are the carefree days of playing tag on the playground, napping on blue vinyl mats, and happily ingesting paste. The kids are onto more complicated activities, like finding their lockers, learning the mind-boggling job of left- versus right-line leader, and religiously letting the classroom hamster out of its cage.

Yes, these are stressful times for kindergartners, but as with all grades from K through 52—depending on if your kid is on the thirty-year college plan—no one suffers more than the parents do.

You can bet our parents were never tortured by the five days designated for "Color of the Week"! Oh, sure, the concept sounds simple enough, but carrying it out turned my military-precision morning routine into total mayhem.

The day the paper came home telling me to dress my child in a different color of the day, for an entire week, I conscientiously taped it on the fridge. Then, like all the other important school papers posted there, I quickly forgot about it. It wasn't until we were outside and the bus came rumbling down the street that my daughter, Jenna, turned to me and said, "Mom, today's Red Day!"

"Oh, really, honey?" I yawned. "That's nice."

"Mom, I'm supposed to wear red!"

I looked down at her white T-shirt and black stretch pants. I ran back inside the house and grabbed the first red thing I could find. As the bus pulled up to the house, I squirted a blob of ketchup on Jenna's shirt.

She glared.

"Tomorrow, I'll do better," I assured her.

I went back in the house, determined to make the next color

day a success. I spent the entire afternoon searching through closets and dresser drawers for something yellow, which was when I made a startling discovery. Jenna's wardrobe was 99.9 percent pink. And there wasn't even a pink day on the sheet!

But, with a little ingenuity, I took an old yellow T-shirt of mine and decided it would make a nice dress. I figured her older sister's yellow hair scrunchy would work perfectly as a belt. The next morning, Jenna was dressed in yellow from her headband right down to her shoelaces.

Jenna looked in the mirror. "I look like a big banana!" She cried.

"Isn't that good?" I asked.

"Everybody's gonna laugh."

I assured her that everyone was going to look like a banana.

When she returned from school that day, she assured me that she was the only one who looked like a fruit.

Green Day posed another problem. In desperation, I pulled a head of lettuce out of the fridge, glued a couple dozen leaves on the front of her T-shirt and pushed her out the door.

She came home with a single leaf clinging to her outfit.

"What happened?" I asked.

"The hamster wouldn't leave me alone."

On Blue Day, I didn't bother looking for the color; instead, I recorded my own CD about a mother who sings the blues BECAUSE HER KID DOESN'T HAVE ANYTHING TO WEAR ON BLUE DAY!

I thought the teacher might take the hint and leave us poor parents alone. Instead, she wrote back, "Dear Mrs. DiSandro, how clever you are! Now I know where Jenna gets her creativity."

The next day was Brown Day. I was so exhausted; I did what any responsible parent would do in the same situation: I kept her home from school.

Color week ended on Friday. I breathed a sigh of relief. Monday morning we'd be back to our semi-mayhem schedule.

"Mom!" Jenna shouted, bursting through the door. "I've got another paper for you!"

The paper read, "It's Homecoming Spirit Week! The dress-up

days are as follows: Monday, Sports Jersey Day; Tuesday, Rainbow Day; Wednesday, Clash Day; Thursday, Stripes and Checks Day . . ."

PROJECT-IMPAIRED PARENTS PLEAD FOR PARDON

Only a short time ago, our family held the naïve notion that the sole purpose of a shoebox was to hold a pair of shoes. But after careful deliberation, during which we turned the box over and examined it from sixty different angles (after our son's teacher said we had to), we discovered a shoebox could be a movie theater.

"Who invented shoeboxes anyway?" I complained to my husband, Tony, as we gathered glue sticks, glue guns, construction paper, and poster board. "Why don't they just sell shoes in a plastic bag? They certainly wouldn't tell our son, Marcus, to make a movie theater out of a plastic bag, now would they?"

Tony glared back at me.

"Yeah, you're right," I agreed. "They probably would."

My husband and I were finally privy to a long-held secret, a secret that my own father uncovered while helping me construct a beaver dam out of milk cartons. As we watched our own son attempt to cut a theater door into the side of a shoebox, we, too, learned the shocking, horrible truth.

School projects are a form of teacher revenge. They congregate in the teachers' lounge, plotting their payback:

"How about the Statue of Liberty made from the crushed shells of 1,000 colored Easter eggs?"

"No, we did that last year."

"Wait, I've got it. We'll have them create an entire town out of shoeboxes. Each family can have a different building."

"Oh, my gosh. That's too cruel!"

"Cruel? Have you forgotten the tarantula Freddy brought for show and tell that wound up in your Coach purse?"

"Yeah, you're right. Shoeboxes it is."

We knew about the project for months, and like all responsible parents, with a strong desire to teach our child the real workings of the business world, we procrastinated. Building construction commenced two days before the due date, after the third written reminder from our boss, uh, I mean our son's teacher.

Gathering at the kitchen table, we contemplated the Herculean task before us. "Last night, I had a terrible nightmare. I opened the shoebox and a genie appeared. I had only one wish and I wasted it on getting rid of the shoebox," I shivered.

"You call that scary?" my husband said. "In my nightmare, I was locked inside the shoebox with Mrs. Cranson, my third-grade teacher, and she sentenced me to an eternity of solving algebra problems."

"Would somebody please help me!" Marcus cried. "I can't do this all by myself!"

So we helped him. Tony covered the shoebox with orange construction paper. I used a marker to draw some lines that remotely resembled bricks. We were cutting a piece of cardboard for the marquee when someone had the nerve to interrupt us.

"Let *me* do something, Dad."

"What was that?" Tony asked, engrossed in his work.

"I didn't hear anything?" I said, positioning the marquee.

"It's me! Your son, Marcus!"

"Can't you see we're busy right now?" I said.

"Let me help," he pleaded.

"Help with what?"

"MY PROJECT!"

So we let Marcus design the ticket booth. He cut a large picture window and put his Lego guy inside. It was the best part of the theater. Then he drew a parking lot on white cardboard and steered one of his Hot Wheels to a choice spot.

We stood back and eyed our masterpiece theater and decided it wasn't half bad. *Jurassic Park* was on a double bill with *Spiderman*.

The next day, Marcus and I proudly placed our theater in the middle of the burgeoning town sprawled throughout the school hallway. I looked around at the other buildings. When I saw a gas station with tiny little pumps constructed out of forged metal, I knew we were in trouble. The Nissan dealership with cars carved from bars of Caress cinched it. And would you believe there was an exact replica of Wrigley Field in Chicago? If it had had lights, I would've sat down and bawled like a baby.

"Mine stinks compared to these other buildings," Marcus said.

"Are you kidding? Yours is just as creative." I lied. "And besides, those kids didn't build those without a lot of help from their parents."

"You guys helped *me*."

"True," I admitted, searching for the proper words to console him. "Now look at Wrigley Field over there, it doesn't even have *lights!*"

Marcus flipped the light switch. The ballpark lit up like a Christmas tree. The lighted scoreboard showed the Cubs leading the Braves, seven to one in the bottom of the eighth. I sat down and bawled like a baby.

So I would like to make this plea to teachers on behalf of project-impaired parents everywhere. Let's cut a deal. We'll promise to keep the insects in our own purses if you vow to keep the shoeboxes for shoes, the milk cartons for milk, the Popsicle sticks for Popsicles, the juice cans for juice . . .

KINDERGARTEN SNITCH OR STITCH

My husband and I breathed a deep sigh of relief. Now that we had the two older children's meetings out of the way, the kindergarten conference would be a cakewalk.

Actually, we were looking forward to Jenna's first parent-teacher conference. Our youngest was so intelligent and intuitive, and, with her fascination for bugs, obviously destined for a career in entomology or with Orkin. We were more than eager to hear what the teacher had to say about our brilliant baby.

We waited impatiently outside the classroom door as the teacher talked to the parents before us. I paced back and forth and glanced at my watch. "It's 7:16!" I said in exasperation. "They've just robbed us of one minute of our time!"

My husband cleared his throat loudly. I coughed. It was an

unspoken conference rule: if the parents before you went over-time, it was your job to let them know as subtly as possible.

At 7:19, I tossed my purse inside the classroom door. "Oops!" I said, retrieving it. "It just slipped out of my hands," I apologized, "at exactly SEVEN NINETEEN!"

The parents stood up to leave. I waved my husband inside. Together, we sat half of ourselves down in the tiny chairs.

"Let's see," Mrs. Williams said, glancing down at her schedule. She looked up smiling. "You're Jenna's parents."

"Yes, we are," we beamed proudly.

Mrs. Williams pulled out Jenna's file. She seemed to be giggling to herself. Then the giggle exploded into laughter. My husband and I exchanged worried glances. Mrs. Williams seemed to be suffering from posttraumatic conference disorder—just our luck for scheduling on the last day.

"Before we look at these papers," she said, attempting to control herself, "I've got to tell you that your daughter is a stitch!"

"A stitch?" I asked.

"She's soooo funny. And the stories she tells about you two," she guffawed, "hysterical!"

My husband and I slid down into our chairs.

"By the way, Mr. DiSandro (giggle), how is your (giggle, giggle) head, since the accident?" Mrs. Williams asked.

"What accident?" my husband asked.

"You know, when you tripped on the ladder rung and dumped the whole can of purple paint on your head?" She said laughing. "Jenna tells the story with such expression."

"I'm sure she does," my husband said.

"And YOU!" Mrs. Williams said, pointing at me. "The way Jenna described how you were screaming, 'Get off my new carpet! Get off my new carpet!' Well, the entire class couldn't stop laughing."

I quickly assured Mrs. Williams this incident had never happened, but she was holding her stomach and didn't seem to hear me.

Taking a deep breath, she asked, "Oh and how is business, Mr. DiSandro? We've heard all about your doughnut shop and how you stumble out of bed at three o'clock in the morning (giggle, giggle), mumbling, 'Got to make the donuts.'"

My husband interrupted, "I don't own a donut shop."

"Oh, we know you don't OWN it, Mr. DiSandro, but everybody has to make a living, right?"

"Excuse me," I interrupted. "My husband is NOT a doughnut maker."

"That's what Jenna says!" she gasped, breaking into a new fit of giggles. My husband shook his head, "Just tell us how Jenna is doing in school?"

"School?"

"Yes, in kindergarten!" I insisted.

"She's doing just fine," Mrs. Williams assured us as she pulled out Jenna's file. "Here is her daily journal. The children are writing and sounding out words all by themselves, so it's sometimes difficult to read. But Jenna can tell you all about it." She pointed to a busy page. "See, this is the two of you hanging the kitchen wallpaper."

"Oh no."

"Oh yes! This is when you threw wallpaper paste at each other and Jenna put you both in a time-out chair. She is just a stitch, isn't she?"

"Just a stitch," we agreed. "Thank you, Mrs. Williams. We're going home to talk to the little snitch, I mean stitch, right now."

"But you still have five minutes of conference time left!" Mrs. Williams shouted to our retreating backs.

My husband sighed. "Oh, well," he said. "If she doesn't go into bugs, she might one day be president of the Liar's Club."

OPERATION GRANDMA

I'm on a mission to help the grandmas of America. Their cupboards and cabinets are stuffed with stuff they can't use and would never buy and it's all because of their cute, seemingly innocent grandchildren.

As soon as school is in full swing, the fundraising forms come home, offering overpriced pizzas, wrapping paper, popcorn, and holiday cheese logs. School officials specifically tell the kids not to sell to strangers and neighbors or go door to door. So the kids take their forms over the river and through the woods, straight to Grandmother's house.

And poor unsuspecting Grandma says, "Sure, I'll order a little something, honey." But after a few grandkids and thirty-three thousand fundraisers, Grandma's house is headed toward foreclosure!

You know the story of *Little Red Riding Hood*, don't you? Actually, the grandma hired the wolf to scare her granddaughter away because she knew she had a fundraiser form for chocolate-covered pretzel sticks stashed under the bread in her basket. And Grandma had just ordered twenty dollars' worth of gourmet popcorn from Red's brother, Little Boy Blue, for his new band uniform, and seed packets for silver bells and cockleshells from her niece, Mary, and a pail of Perrier from Jack and Jill!

But at least she wasn't as bad off as her poor sister, Old Mother Hubbard. Hubbard's daughter was the lady who lived in the shoe. Mother Hubbard had so many grandchildren showing up on her doorstep with order forms that she didn't know what to do! She couldn't even buy her poor dog a bone! And now you know the *rest* of these stories.

So as you can see, this problem's been going on for some time. Somebody's got to do something. So in a campaign called Operation Grandma, I'm out to stop the fundraising madness before Grandma goes broke.

First, I'm putting out a tip sheet to help grandmas spot the persuasive propaganda employed by today's grandkids:

1. Beware if your grandchild suddenly starts giving you gushing compliments like, "My Grandma, you look less wrinkly today."

2. Beware of a sudden concern for your health: "Grandma, you're looking so thin and drawn. I have just the thing to fatten you up—page 47, a holiday fruitcake. You buy two for only $49.99!"

3. Keep your glasses on at all times, even when you're sleeping! The last grandma who took hers off thought she was signing up to join the Bobby Vinton fan club and instead wound up with sixty decorative tins filled with cheese doodles.

Along with the tip sheets, I'm writing a letter to the schools. If we must have a fundraiser, at least fill the forms with items Grandma can use, like a decorative box of denture cream or a can of Metamucil that comes in red and green granules for the holidays?

Let's put some things on there Grandma really cares about, like bingo markers, lottery tickets, and Jack Daniels. Okay, I'm just kidding. Grandmas would rather have the bingo stampers, not the markers.

And last, I'm starting a nationwide television campaign. It will feature a group of grandmas with armbands that show a pizza with a big X through it. Standing shoulder to shoulder, they'll face down a bunch of grandkids in the middle of the street. The caption will read, "JUST SAY NO!"

Yup, I'll be starting Operation Grandma any day now. I just need a little start-up capital. So as soon as my mom sends me the twenty dollars she owes me for wrapping paper, I'll be all set.

NOTES ON GRADUATION

Like a tidal wave, the familiar music washed over me as the eager, young graduates poured out into the sunshine. They marched to the same rhythm as I and many others had done before them, while the tassels from their white caps danced in the summer wind.

As if they were precariously carrying books atop their heads, their hands often reached out for balance. The sight of these tentative, yet eager, steps seemed eerily familiar to those of us standing on the sideline—watching. We can no longer reach out to steady them or come to their rescue should they tumble to the ground. Today, we can merely watch as they file past.

The camera trembles beneath my fingers. The circle in the center of the viewfinder scans the procession, searching for its focus. Girls giggle and boys shuffle into view, some hanging their heads in embarrassment of the seemingly corny pomp and circumstance, others standing taller, shooting for the sun, as bold as the dandelions dotting the lawn.

Then, there, right there, behind the boy with the goofy grin, the circle frames the blond with the dimpled smile—CLICK—a picture of my daughter. I chuckle, as if I need a photo to remember this moment. It is already seared in my mind and my heart along with so many others before it: my daughter stomping boldly up the school-bus steps on her first day of school, perched atop the stepstool at the kitchen stove while cooking her first macaroni-and-cheese dinner, flirting dangerously with her first love.

Where have all the year's gone? I wondered. Wasn't it just last week I had taped her first finger painting on the refrigerator door? Wasn't it only yesterday that I reached for her hand to cross the street? It was, I'm certain, only a moment ago that I rocked her to sleep in my arms.

As she marches by, so grown-up and filled with knowledge, I hold back the urge to run up and yank her out of line. I want to tie her shoes and pull her shiny hair into girlish pigtails in a last-ditch effort to let her know I still matter. "You still need me!" I want to shout.

I can hear the muffled cries of all the other parents as we clap on cue, as our children file past, as our cameras attempt to capture the fleeting moment.

Life is full of beginnings and endings, and for a parent and child, sometimes they become so entangled and intertwined, we're uncertain where one begins and another leaves off. There's a pulling and pushing to break free and those same desperate motions are too often used to hold on and hold tight.

As our children file past to collect one more token of their independence, we can only stand on the sidelines watching. Only watching.

The ceremony sped by as quickly as the camera stored each still shot, advancing with a whirring sound, announcing itself ready to record the next stage of my daughter's life, no matter how badly I might want to stop it, or at least slow the shutter to a speed I could handle.

Afterward, my daughter and I slowly disentangled ourselves from the crowd. With my emotions threatening to cloud this sunny day, I somehow managed to whisper, "I'm proud of you."

She smiled back at me. Her blue eyes shimmered so radiantly

in the afternoon sunlight that I gasped for air. I quickly looked away as we walked across the parking lot, not wanting her to see the emotions I could no longer hide.

Suddenly, I felt her reach for my hand.

I wrapped my fingers around hers, but not too tightly.

My daughter is wise beyond her years. I suppose graduating from kindergarten will do that to a person.

CHAPTER 4

Scores As Supersupporter

For the parents of a Little Leaguer, a baseball game is simply a nervous breakdown into innings. —Earl Wilson

BARBIE STRIKES OUT!

If I had only ditched Barbie for a baseball every once in a while, I wouldn't be in this current predicament. Had I paid more attention to the play by play of a major-league game instead of investing all my talent and energy into selecting the perfect ensemble for a day at Barbie's Beach House, I might be better prepared. But when the kids on my block were sliding into second or rounding third, Barbie and I were packing for a trip to France.

How was I to know that one day I would actually grow up, get married, and have kids and a body not like Barbie's, but closer in proportions to my Voyager minivan? And that instead of jetting to Europe, I would be standing in the middle of a baseball field trying to catch a curve ball, a screw ball, or any ball for that matter! A straight one, a fast one, even that one bouncing off my foot. Oops! I missed it.

"Don't worry, Marcus." I shout to my impatient son. "I'll catch the next one. Oops! Well, okay, then maybe the next one. Could you throw it slower?" I beg.

"Any slower, Mom, and I could run out there and catch it myself."

"Okay, okay. Why don't you get your bat and I'll shoot some balls to you."

"PITCH! Mom! It's PITCH some . . . OOOWWW!"

"Sorry, Marcus. Bad pitch. Here comes another one."

"OOOWWW!"

"Come on, Marcus. I didn't hit you that time."

"No," my son said shaking his head. "You hit that lady over there on that bench."

"Just shake it off, lady. Nice slacks, by the way!"

Thanks to Barbie, I possess the athletic skills of a cross-eyed gnat. As game time draws near, I impart my meager nuggets of baseball wisdom: "Now remember, Marcus. If the ball is coming toward you, move out of the way so you don't get hurt, honey. And tuck your shirt in, Ken, I mean, Marcus!"

As I take my place in the bleachers, I resist the urge to go over, straighten Marcus's cap, and pull his left pant leg down. Those Barbie days resurface when you least expect it.

"Marcus!" I shout.

He swings! He misses. He turns to glare at me.

"Straighten your pant leg!" I shout across the field.

Soon, Marcus is heading back to his seat. As I understand it, my son was out without even hitting the ball.

"Is that good?" I ask the father sitting next to me.

"Not unless your son was on the other team," he explained while edging down the bleacher in the other direction.

Marcus and his team lost the game that day, and the game after that, and the game after that. And with each loss the team racked up, I learned a little more about baseball. I now know the difference between a ball and a strike. I understand that it's better to hit than to miss. I can tell a foul ball from a fair ball. And I can even decipher when the umpire is wrong about a call. "My son was safe, you nearsighted buffoon!!"

But having never played the sport, there's one thing I can't help with and that's losing five straight games in a row. The tears are unstoppable and the crying, though understandable, is almost embarrassing.

"I don't get it. Our pitching is improving. We're fielding better than ever. It's not fair!"

"I know it's tough. But remember, it's not whether you win or lose, it's how you play the game, Mom."

"You're right, son," I sob, wiping the tears from my eyes. "Thanks for reminding me. Can we go for ice cream?"

"Sure, Mom. But you've got to promise me one thing. At the next game, wear something besides that Barbie cheerleading outfit?"

"Can I still bring my pompoms?" I pleaded.

My son replied, "Not unless you want to cheer from inside the van."

ONE PITCH AND YOU'RE OUCH!

My son is no longer a Pinto, which means I am no longer a Pinto mom cheering in the stands. Instead, I'm inside the Little League dugout pleading with my son to take up chess. Gone forever are the carefree days of the Pinto League, when the coaches pitched to their own team players.

In Pinto, the coaches lobbed the ball nice and easy, directly over the plate. They zeroed in on the sweet spot on the bat so precisely that if a batter even sneezed he connected with the ball.

Now, my son's old enough for the Mustang League, which means that during a game there's one primary thought running through the minds of the infielders and outfielders, coaches and parents, one notion dominating the minds of the kids at the concession booth and the elderly man watering his lawn across the street: "PLEASE DON'T LET THE PITCHER HURT ME TODAY!"

In the Mustang League, the only safe spot at game time is on the pitcher's mound. Unfortunately, you must be nine or ten years old to secure that coveted position. The rest of us take cover wherever we can find it.

My son usually plays the outfield. Thankfully, he doesn't see any action out there, because the vast majority of players are walked. And if by chance the pitcher manages to get a ball in the strike zone, the batter, in most cases, neglects to swing because he's sitting safely in the family van in the parking lot until the umpire calls, "Ball four!"

But after most pitches, you hear a loud thud, followed by a gut-wrenching scream and the coach saying, "Shake it off, buddy, and take first base."

The bases are loaded with injured walkers unsuccessfully trying to shake it off. And if a player somehow manages to drag his battered body across home plate, he brings in a run. The fathers cheer from the stands, proud of their son's first limping steps into manhood. It's the real-men-play-hurt step, also known as the don't-let-'em-see-your-pain-until-you-get-home-to-mommy step.

While the fathers applaud and high-five, the mothers stand near the dugout, with gurneys, ready to transport the wounded to nearby rescue vehicles. As the moms apply first aid and ice packs, their terrified sons confess their deepest fears.

"I hate baseball! I wouldn't care if I never saw another baseball zooming toward my head in my whole life!" my own son admits. It didn't help that he was whacked in the face by the very first pitch, in the very first practice of the season.

When we mothers see the fear in our babies' eyes, we want to scoop them up in our warm, protective arms and run out of the park without looking back. But our motherly intuition knows what they really need to hear. They want our reassurance. They want us to say, "Yes, I'm certain you'll live past ten and a half. And if you keep your eye on the ball, you will be able to read the pitch and know whether to swing or get out of the way." So this is what I say as I grudgingly walk my son back to the field so he can pick up his bat with a little more confidence.

Of course, it doesn't hurt to have a little talk with the pitcher now and then either: "Listen up, kid. If you hurt my baby, *you'll* never see ten and a half!"

CONCESSION AT THE CONCESSION STAND

It goes without saying that organized sports are a good way for your kids to learn about team playing and sportsmanship. They learn discipline, routine, and how not to give up when the score is ten to zip—or at least how not to cry their eyes out when the other team is looking. But there is one drawback those involved neglect to tell you. One reason why it's not such a grand idea to sign your kid up for, let's say, baseball. After about a year, everyone, including the resident gopher on field number two, will come to realize that you're the only parent on the entire eighty-team league who hasn't signed up to work the concession stand.

While contentedly munching on a hot dog, slathering your nachos in cheese, and slurping down an extra-large icy fruit drink, you overhear some parents complaining about the mom in the front-row bleachers.

"Look at her over there, scarfing down concession-stand food without even an ounce of guilt. For skirting her tour of duty, she should be forbidden to eat the fruits of our labor."

You finally get the idea that they're talking about you when they combine your name with a word I won't mention and aim popcorn and pretzel pieces at your head. So to show your commitment to the team, you graciously walk over and, without hesitation, sign your husband up for concession duty.

At least, that's what I did. Then he claimed he had to work late, and suddenly, I find myself in the middle of a mess hall, with a small curly-haired fireball named Susie—Drill Sergeant Susie—chief operating officer of the concession stand. After she leaves here, I'm certain she'll be taking over for Colin Powell.

Susie gave her small band of enlisted the once-over and barked, "Don't tell me your name, because I won't remember it!" Pointing to her crew, she said, "You and you, work the window. And you," she added, squinting her eyes and nodding her chin in my direction, "you're the cook!"

"Me??" I gasped. "But . . . but I purposely signed my son up for baseball so I wouldn't have to cook on Fridays. Why can't I work the window?"

She guffawed. "Hah! I saw your math transcripts. You can't *handle* the window! Training begins in five minutes. Go wash your hands!"

I considered going AWOL, but then the hot dogs boiled over and sarge yelled, "Cook! Turn down those dogs!"

"Aye-aye, sir."

Susie leapt over the counter to begin my training. "Listen up. You wrap hot dogs in silver paper like this."

"Piece of cake."

"You need to keep sixteen in the warmer at all times."

"Sixteen?!"

"And nobody likes a squished dog, so be GENTLE!" she barked. "If they wanna pita pocket," she continued, "you ask, 'Pepperoni or ham and cheese?' Try it."

"Uh, we have pepperoni or ham and cheese."

"YELL!"

"Pepperoni or . . ."

"LOUDER!"

I tried it again.

Her curls shook like little spikes. "Hopeless."

"By the way," I asked, trying to make conversation, "did you ever hear of the Soup Nazi?"

"He's my cousin!" she spat. "Here, spritz and dip the pretzels, microwave for three minutes, the pita pockets two minutes and twenty seconds, the mini-pizzas four minutes. We have hamburgers. No cheeseburgers!" Susie took the cover off the Crockpot. "And this is for Walking Taco."

"Walking Taco," I laughed.

"No laugh! This is our best seller." Susie turned and shouted to the workers in front. "Open the window and let the selling begin."

"Wait," I cried. "I'm not ready. How many minutes on the pita? I don't have sixteen hot dogs, and . . ."

The wooden doors slapped open. You could hear the stomping of 3,002 little feet as the T-ball players ascended. Of course, we couldn't see them except for the blip of a second when their heads barely cleared the window as they jumped up to shout out their order. Sometimes it took a few jumps.

(Jump) "Uh (jump), Mars (jump) Bar (jump), please." Ordering was more exercise than the actual game.

Fortunately for me, the T-ball tykes were interested in candy.

Suddenly Sergeant Susie poked her head in the window. "Incoming! Incoming! Junior League just finished. Man your stations!"

For the next half-hour I walked tacos, pita-d pockets, and

wrapped hot dogs, hamburgers—no cheeseburgers—and sliced mini-pizzas.

Susie marched over to inspect my station. She looked into the hamburger warmer. "That's not how you stack the hamburgers! But wait a minute," she said after examining it closer. Then she looked back at me. "This might be better than the way we do it now." She eyed me with a new respect. "What did you say your name was?"

"My na—"

"Nevermind! I won't remember it."

AM I AN ATHLETIC SUPPORTER?

The pressure to succeed at organized sports is really getting out of hand. You can read the signs of mental and physical stress all over the faces of the competitors—tears, fear, anger.

They kick, they cry, they scream, and sometimes when their immaturity gets the best of them, they even throw things.

"Here's your shin guards, Lauren!"

"Ouch! That hurt, mom!"

"I *told* you they were in the laundry room. Now we have only six minutes to get to soccer practice."

We wash, drive, watch, cheer, patch, support, listen, coach, and counsel. We daily check and recheck schedules, outline maps, and consult our watches so as not to drop the ball. We're expected to know the whereabouts of our children's socks, uniforms, etc., at all times.

"Mom, have you seen my cup?"

"Gee, I don't think I used it last, Marcus, but let me check. Oh, here it is. Looks like Champ chewed it for dinner last night."

During dinner, I notice we're falling behind, so I inform the troops. "Okay, everybody, listen up! We have to finish eating this meal at 17:00 sharp! I need to drive Marcus to baseball practice at 5:15, come back home, and get Lauren for soccer at 5:30 P.M. We all have to pitch in, here. Chew faster! Faster! Faster!"

Yes, I'm a baseball mom and a soccer mom. But after a few seasons of both, I'd much rather be a chess mom. I'm positive that during chess matches no one ever shouts, "Get an ice pack!" or, another commonly heard phrase, "I just saw lightning!"

"No you didn't, Mrs. DiSandro," the ref informs me, "that was just the sun glinting off your parka."

"What sun?" I shivered. "I haven't seen any sun! All I can see is my breath and the icicles dangling from my nose. Call the game, *please*!!"

But they never call a soccer game.

Did it ever occur to anyone that the Midwest and soccer go together like plaid and paisley, chocolate and potato chips, beer and cherry pie? (Wait, a minute, I've tried that; it's not bad, really. The foam makes a great topping.)

Everyone knows, especially meteorologists, that you can't predict the weather in the Midwest in fall or spring. You can begin a game in 90 degrees and have an igloo forming over the goalie by the time the final whistle blows.

While shivering on the cold, metal bleachers, a dad saunters over and magically pulls a mini-sized La-Z-Boy out of his hip pocket and sits down. He plugs in a heater, pulls out the paper, and relaxes. His wife is the soccer coach. She yells plays from the sidelines with a six month old strapped to her back.

I'm lucky if I can remember Treat Day! Whenever they pass the volunteer sign-up sheet, I always feel like a real loser for checking NO, so I write in, "Just had back surgery."

The coach's kid is the one kicking sixty goals per game. Of course, how your child plays is no reflection on you. It's merely a coincidence that I happened to be hiding in the Porta-Potty when my daughter, the goalie, let five goals go by in the first five seconds of the game.

Sometimes you have two games at the same time and the supportive parents split up. But the kids are so understanding:

"You always loved Marcus best. That's why you went to *his* game instead of mine," the middle daughter cries.

"But, Lauren, they were at the exact same time. What did you want me to do, rent a plane and parachute onto the sidelines during halftime?"

"Yes."

"Well, I checked that and some other parent beat me to it."

When it comes to encouraging your child from the sidelines, you have to find the acceptable level of enthusiasm, which lies somewhere between cheering like a lunatic and appearing almost comatose.

"You didn't cheer, mom!" my oldest complains.

"Marcus, you told me not to."

"Yeah, but I didn't really mean it."

But it's all about sportsmanship, right? And discipline. And if our kids stick with it, we're positive they'll get a scholarship to college. Nevermind that, after sixteen years of paying for sports, we could've paid for college *twice*!

So let's play ball! Unless, of course, someone starts an organized stationery-bicycle team. Sign us up.

MOM GETS A KICK OUT OF KARATE

My daughter is taking karate and you should be very afraid. She's a yellow belt. Before that, she was a white belt. Each belt has all these colorful stripes. I have no idea what any of these belts or stripes mean, but I must say they complement any outfit. I do know that her goal is to get a black belt, and since black goes with everything, I think she's made a wise choice.

It all began when my daughter, Lauren, brought me this newspaper ad that read, "Ever since I joined karate, my room is always clean."

Now, you might think it ludicrous that my husband and I would pay seventy dollars a month for my daughter to keep her room clean, but, then, you haven't seen her room. Actually, I thought the seventy dollars included a person who would come over and clean her room, but unfortunately, that hasn't happened.

But other things are happening. She's changing and I can't quite put my finger on it. At home, she strikes all these poses and punches the air with purpose. She looks tough, really tough, and yet graceful.

Before we leave for karate, something awfully strange takes

place. If she sees that her uniform is wrinkled—I am not kidding—she irons it! Yes, my preteen can actually *see* the wrinkles!

When she walks into the karate studio, she bows. When she meets her instructor, she bows. She shows respect to her fellow students. They must follow a code of conduct an arm long. They have a student creed, which kids are to memorize, that reads:

> I will behave in a way that will make my karate school and my family happy.
>
> I will be true to my karate school and what it teaches.
>
> I will be honest and help my parents, my teachers, and my friends.
>
> I will not hit. I will only use karate in protecting myself or my family.

(I immediately went home and wrote up a family creed. Now I just need the karate instructors to come over and make my kids follow it.)

When my daughter, Lauren, earns another stripe, she walks out of the karate studio with her head held high. According to the instructor, the stripes are earned when the students learn another one of the self-defense moves, each a blend of the Kyukyu Kempo and Modern Arnis styles.

I know nothing about martial arts, but I do know that they've shown Lauren how to defend herself if she's grabbed from behind. They've shown her the places on a body that will bring a person to the ground. She can kick as high as any cheerleader. She can do something to a shoulder that could make a grown person cry. And they've shown her how to make these grunting noises that scare our dog to death.

Of course, the question in the back of my mind is, will all these moves work if my beautiful, young daughter is attacked? If you've ever seen the Pink Panther movies, Inspector Clouseau has a houseboy that is instructed to attack him by surprise anytime, anywhere. I'd like to try that, but I'm afraid. Her older brother is afraid too. We've seen her practice, and, well, we make a point not to surprise her these days.

I'm hoping the repetition of doing these moves for months on end will unconsciously kick in when they have to, even if she is terrified. I'm hoping that the punches that now meet only air will connect with force. I'm hoping she'll kick where it counts and bring the attacker to the ground writhing in agony.

If karate can do all that, frankly, I don't care what her room looks like.

RISK TAKING IS ALL WET

Well, you know me, always talking about courage and taking risks and such. So it shouldn't surprise anyone that at a house by the lake one weekend, when my friend's husband, Scott, asked, "Who wants to try water-skiing?", I piped right up and said, "Me!"

Unfortunately, nature's elements worked against me. It was too cold, the water was too choppy, and the wind was blowing in the wrong direction. And when I realized I'd actually have to put on my bathing suit, well, let's just say I didn't want to terrify all those cute little woodland creatures.

In other words, I came to my senses. So I strode back toward the house to have a second helping of homemade strawberry shortcake, when I heard the boat engine roar. I turned around to see two of my babies getting into the boat with two traitors—my husband and Scott.

I waddled toward the boat, "What are you two doing?" I clucked to my baby chicks.

"Water-skiing," they answered, settling into their seats.

"But you've never done it before," I reminded them. "Now get out of there and I'll cut you up some strawberry short—"

"Mom," my eldest interrupted, "you're always telling us to try new things. You're the one who said, 'You must do the thing you think you cannot do.'"

"That wasn't me. That was some senile old lady named Eleanor Roosevelt. Besides," I added, "I was talking about math problems not water-skiing."

The boat was pulling away, so I did what any mother hen in my situation would do. I quickly hopped aboard so that if something awful happened, I could assure my husband it was all his fault.

In the middle of the lake, my son, Marcus, plopped into the water. He bobbed around in his life jacket, teeth chattering, while they handed him the skis. Only his own mother could see the terror beneath his pale blue smile.

"Boy, I didn't think he'd be this scared," Scott whispered.

I watched while Marcus struggled to get the huge flat boards strapped to his feet. It took a while, so everyone else took a nap.

Finally, Marcus was ready to give it a try.

"Keep your ski tips up," Scott instructed him. He revved the boat into gear.

Suddenly, a terrified cry stopped him. "Wait! Wait! I'm not ready!"

Everyone glared at the big chicken. "Okay, okay," I said. "I'm ready." This time, I kept my thoughts to myself and sat in silent terror as my son was pulled up and out of the water. I then gasped as he immediately nosedived right back into it.

"Marcus, let go of the rope!" Scott yelled. "Don't want to drag him around the lake," he chuckled.

How could he chuckle at a time like this? "Good try, Marcus," I yelled. "Now get back in the boat." But to my dismay, he wanted to do it again. While we tracked down the floating skis and Marcus put them on again, the sun almost set.

Positioning himself behind the boat, Marcus was pulled again. And this time, to our amazement, he didn't nosedive into the water! He teetered for a half-second and then tottered into the water!

"I'm done," he announced when he resurfaced.

Breathing a deep sigh of relief, I said, "That's enough for one day." But then I felt someone pouting over my left shoulder.

"Don't I get to try?" my twelve-year-old baby chick squeaked.

"No!" I barked. "Didn't you see your brother? It's too hard."

Scott, having three daughters of his own, wasn't about to see Lauren miss out. "Well, it's getting late, but let's give her a chance."

To avoid the nine-hour ski fitting, they stuck Lauren in the skis while she was still on the boat and then slid her off into the water. She easily located the rope and Scott began pulling. Lauren surfaced and actually looked like she was skiing before she fell back into the water.

Our boat rocked with cheers. Other boaters flocked around us.

"What happened? Did she do a backflip?" one boater asked.

"No," I bragged. "She almost got up!"

Once back on shore, my children couldn't contain their excitement.

"Wow, that was so cool!" Marcus said. "I can't wait to try it again."

"Me too!" chimed in Lauren. "I was scared, but I'm sure glad I did it."

"Yeah," agreed Marcus. "It was awesome."

It seems failure never felt so good.

I didn't say a word. I just sat there proudly fluffing my feathers.

A SPORT A MOM CAN RUN WITH

I've watched my kids play in every sport made since the ball was invented. Through torrential rains, hurricane winds, and blinding snow, I've chauffeured, cheered, and encouraged, and wished my kids had taken up chess. But since Bobby Fischer is missing, along with my kids' chess skills, I've finally found an alternative spectator sport that I can revel in.

It's as fast paced as basketball, as nail-biting as baseball, as competitive as soccer, and yet, by the time it takes the ref to call a foul, the pitcher to throw a strike, or the goalie to get in position, it's all over. That's right, instead of an all-day, bring-your-breakfast-lunch-stadium seat-and-all weather poncho event, this sport, from start to finish, lasts, oh, about seventeen minutes and twenty-four seconds! Not that I'm counting.

Usually, the games take place on a Saturday morning, but not too early, so you have plenty of time to get your coffee and doughnut. When you pull up to the park, your kid goes off to meet his team. You can easily tell from your car when you need to walk over, pat your kid on the back, and, while munching on your powdered, cream-filled doughnut, mumble, "Good luck!"

It's a tense a half-second, then BOOM! A gun goes off. Your coffee shakes and the ground rumbles as your son and two hundred other kids start running.

As the parent, your duties are over for the next sixteen minutes and twenty-four seconds! You don't have to worry about your kid missing a pop fly, losing the jump ball, or getting crushed by a linebacker. The most common injury is a pulled hamstring. So you leisurely saunter over to the finish line. On your way there, you may see your kid pass by on his first lap around the park. You lean in close and shout, "Run! Run!" or "Faster! Faster!" or "Let's do lunch!"

It doesn't really matter. He can't see or hear you. He's too busy sweating, gasping for air, and wishing he'd taken up chess.

The excitement builds as you take your place along the flagged rope. This is the spot where the runners cross the finish line and it's the only other place you're expected to do something. A few minutes later, the kids start running in and you say, "GO! GO!", as powdered sugar spews from your lips.

What a riveting seventeen minutes and twenty-four seconds it has been! Your kid is keeling over from exhaustion as you pat him on the back. And no matter where he's placed, you can't go wrong by saying, "It looked like you were really running out there!" Your kid nods or passes out for a second; it's hard to tell which is happening with that drool hanging from his mouth.

Now, you can either stay another five minutes to see the rest of the kids come gasping in, or you can leave. That's right, I said leave! It's over. The day has just begun and you're done with your kid's sport!

You're so happy you consider running back to the car, but you catch yourself. You don't want to pull a hamstring. Besides, it's hard to run while carrying your sixteen-year-old kid on your back.

CHAPTER 5

Prevails Over Perils with Pets

Recently my friend and I had an argument because he tried to tell me that looking after his dog, Pepper, was just as difficult as taking care of my then-two-year-old Alexandra. I wish I was still punching him.—Ray Ramono, from *Everything and a Kite*

RESPONSIBILITY SMELLS A LITTLE FISHY

The poster is to blame. The warm, fuzzy poster with the cute, curly headed kid sitting on the banks of a picturesque pond, dipping his pint-sized fishing pole into the water. It spoke to me: *Give your children a fish and they eat for a day, teach them to fish and they eat for a lifetime.*

I replied, "Are you saying that I need to teach my children financial responsibility?"

The poster said, "Yes, haven't you ever heard of a metaphor?"

So I gave my kids a few thoughtfully chosen chores (those being the ones I hated doing, like cleaning the toilets and taking out the smelly garbage) and rewarded their efforts with a few bucks.

Then one day, at the breakfast table, my son announced, "I saved enough money to buy two chameleons."

"That's nice, honey," I said, ignoring him like I do every morning.

"Can we get them after school?"

"Sure," I said. "By the way, what's a chameleon? A new trading card?"

"No, it's a lizard."

"A WHAAAAT?!"

"Haven't you noticed the aquarium set up in my bedroom?" he asked.

"I thought you were growing plants," I said taking an extra-big gulp of coffee and realizing the serious nature of this discussion. "Nice, quiet plants without teeth."

"Mom, you promised we could use our spending money any way we wanted." he insisted.

"I said THAT?"

"You sure did," my daughter, Lauren, chimed in. It seems Lauren had enough money for two goldfish.

We entered the pet store filled with other dumbstruck parents and kids wielding the deadliest of weapons—discretionary income. I had hoped discretionary meant that Marcus and Lauren would spend their money according to *my* discretion. Now, I could only hope that all the other kids had already scooped up all the choice reptiles.

Suddenly, Marcus shouted, "There they are!"

"Don't show them to me!" I said, backing away. "Just have the clerk put them in a black, steel-plated box, where they'll stay until Dad gets home."

The clerk deposited the creatures in a see-through bag, one even a goldfish could wiggle its way out.

"Now, where's the lizard food?" my son asked.

"Over there in that aquarium," the clerk said, nodding toward a busy tank.

"But there are live, crawly, disgusting things in that tank," I pointed out.

"Yup, crickets," the clerk chuckled, obviously enjoying my dismay.

"Great, but we need lizard food. You know," I explained, "like Puppy Chow. It comes in a bag and you just pour it into a bowl. We need Chameleon Chow."

"Crickets," she stated. "Chameleons eat live crickets, about a dozen a week."

"I have enough allowance for that," Marcus quickly calculated.

That night, while I stood outside trembling and cursing the day I read that poster, the lizards moved in with dad's help. *Maybe Marcus could teach the chameleons how to fish for their own crickets*, I thought.

The next day while making Marcus's bed (Hey, I could deduct fifty cents of his allowance for it—less discretionary income means fewer pets), I decided to sneak a peek at his new roommates, Herb and Gladys. I peeked, I peered, and I screamed: "MARCUS, YOUR LIZARDS ARE LOOSE!"

Marcus raced up the stairs, glanced into his aquarium, and said, "No they aren't, Mom. They're still in there."

"Where?" I asked from my vantage point on top of his dresser.

"Herb's hanging from the green ivy and Gladys is on the rock."

"How come I can't see them?" I asked suspiciously.

"Because they're chameleons. They change colors to match their surroundings."

Sure, kind of like politicians, I thought—and secretly christened them Gore and Bush. The chameleons looked dead even when they were alive, which is more than I could say for Lauren's fish.

"Mom, something's wrong with Courtney," Lauren announced. "She's laying like this." Lauren proceeded to lay on the kitchen floor with her back arched and her head tilted to one side.

"By any chance is Courtney laying upside down on TOP of the water?" I asked.

"Yeah."

"Well, she's dead."

Lauren was devastated—for an entire second. Then she asked, "Can I get another one?" In the next few weeks, Lauren helped more goldfish meet their maker than Dr. Kevorkian did.

"What smells in here?" I'd ask during nightly prayers.

"It's my new fishies," Lauren stated matter of factly. "They're dead."

"Did you feed them?"

"A whole can of fish food," she assured me.

"Well, at least we know they didn't starve to death."

"Can I get some more?"

"Lauren, those little guys are onto you," I warned her. "Whenever we walk into the pet store, they crouch behind the nearest seaweed plant!"

Eventually, as with all live pets, my children lost interest. Now, my maternal instincts are invested in keeping them from the customary toilet funeral. But there is some good news to report. Gore is going to be a mother.

A CREATURE IS STIRRING

The problem with family meetings is that your children often present detailed reports on why they should own live pets. And since the irrational members now outnumber the rational in our household (They counted baby Jenna's burp as a vote in their favor), we now have a hamster. Well, my daughter, Lauren, has a hamster. The rest of us have wood shavings in our hair and there are tiny black specks all over the house—specks that look like lint from our black socks but, upon picking them up and rolling them between our fingers, we discover ("YUCH!") they're actually hamster droppings.

Lauren aptly named her white and gray rodent, Nibbles, because we soon discovered Nibbles could effortlessly chew his way out of a bank vault. The first week, Nibbles lived in Lauren's room in a plastic condo as roomy as my mother's townhome. It had bedrooms, hallways, even it's own groundskeeper—my husband.

Nibbles soon engaged in normal, annoying hamster behavior. Lauren neglected to mention in her report that hamsters are nocturnal. He gnawed, nested, and scratched his way into our nightly dreams.

"What was that?" My husband said, grabbing for the light switch but finding my head instead.

"Ouch!" I cried. Rubbing my head, I yawned and climbed out of bed to close Lauren's door.

Nibbles nibbled his way out and opened it.

There was only one family member who seemed to enjoy Nibbles' nightly escapades, Baby Jenna. Nibbles and Jenna became instant friends. Here was someone she could relate to—someone else who slept all day and partied all night, a buddy with the same three goals, eating, chewing, and . . . well, let's just say we called them the dynamic doo-doo duo.

For Jenna and Nibbles, it became a nightly contest to see who could stay awake the longest. Jenna dribbled. Nibbles nibbled. Jenna cried. Nibbles nibbled. Nibbles was relegated to the basement. Of course, we couldn't do that with Jenna, although for one moment of insanity, we considered it.

Obviously, Nibbles wasn't pleased with his new digs. One night soon after, Nibbles moved out, or more accurately, chewed out.

There were only 30,000 possible places he could hide in our basement, and we looked in every one of them. Then we called the pet store and thanked them for neglecting to tell us that hamsters find their forty-dollar condos quite tasty if they lack something else to chew on.

My husband finally found him. He was hanging out on the wrong side of the basement with a bad gang of mice, smoking cigarettes, and wearing baggy pants and an earring. We had to enroll him in a tough-love program before he agreed to come back home to his clean, Habitrail living.

No one sleeps too easily now that we know Nibbles can get out.

I imagine him nibbling at my feet. Marcus imagines a drive-by mouse shooting. My husband just sleeps with the cover over his face. Jenna calls for him all night long. And Lauren knows Nibbles is quickly nibbling his way into a foster home.

But it's almost Christmas, so I'll be generous and give him one more chance.

Now, I'm trying to teach him to take a bottle from the fridge and give Jenna her middle-of-the-night feeding. If he can master that, he can stay as long as he wants.

POST-PUPPY PUDDLES

"See, Champ?" I said with all the enthusiasm of a high-school cheerleader. "Everybody's doing it. Doberman's do it. Dachshund's do it. Poodles do it. Even you can do it!"

Champ and I were sitting on the front stoop, watching all his neighborhood friends "going."

According to a recent article, owning a pet can lower high blood pressure and reduce stress. However, the article neglected to mention that trying to coax your new pet to "go," will increase your stress to a level high enough to blow up the blood-pressure machine at Walgreen's.

The article also stated that pets could increase the survival rate for people with heart problems. Personally, I never had a heart problem until I witnessed my new pet decorating the ninety-dollar imitation Persian rug in my hallway.

"Now, watch that collie," I informed him. "She goes straight to her business. No fooling around, no sniffing the same tree for six hours."

I was impressed. Champ was impressed, too—with my shoelace.

I steered him toward the backyard to introduce him to his potty place. To my amazement, Champ ran directly to the nearest tree and started eating it.

So after an hour, I took him inside where Champ ran directly to the nearest table leg and started to "go."

Of course, there were a few times when Champ actually did "go" outside. Then I gave him a treat and jumped around the backyard like a lunatic, squeaking, "Good boy, good boy!" And just to be sure he knew how happy I was about his success, I tossed off a couple of cartwheels and a backflip. Later, a neighbor stopped by to ask whether my medication was by prescription or over the counter.

Obviously, she didn't own a pet.

The article went on to say that, "Pet owners make fewer visits to the doctor." That's because pet owners are too busy calling the vet!

After my fifteenth call, the vet said that maybe I was too nervous and the dog sensed it. I was supposed to examine whether there were any other issues that might interfere with training.

There was another issue. I was trying to comprehend how I had arrived at this moment in my life, where my deepest desire was to witness a dog do its doo-doo.

Getting a dog was supposed to help my children deal with the trauma of moving from one state to another. But the only one suffering from traumatic stress syndrome was me. The kids were busy playing with their new friends.

We had taken a pre-pet class a few months back and now the instructor's warning echoed in my ear: "Don't get a dog to teach your kids responsibility. Moms take care of dogs. MOMS TAKE CARE OF DOGS!"

I had ignorantly assumed that my kids would be different. (*Note: Never, ever assume your kids will be different.*) My kids were going to shoulder the responsibility and be this dog's mommy and daddy. We even had a signed contract. But Champ ate it.

It's not that the kids weren't helping. They had primary scooper duty. And when they came home from school, they eagerly took Champ out, after I remind them how badly they wanted this dog in the first place! But they quickly realized the awesome responsibility caring for a puppy requires and they copped out on being doggie parents.

According to the dog instructor, puppies require a new mother image for security. Apparently, I'm the only one who fits the job description. I haven't combed my hair in days, I need a shower, and I'm crabby from getting up in the middle of the night. Now, I know exactly what the problem is. I'm suffering from a severe case of post-puppy blues.

EMPTY NEST SYNDROME

I recently dreamed about the family rodent and woke up on my hands and knees, calling his name down the heater vent. "Nibbles? Nibbles, are you there? Come home to mommy!"

You see, that's the problem with pets. No matter what type of creature the kids bring home, as a mother, your nurturing instincts automatically kick in, and suddenly, you find yourself bonding with a member of the rodent family. Sure, he looks like a rat and has incisors that could clip off a couple of fingers for breakfast, but he's a member of your family. And you begin to worry about whether he has enough to eat and spend entire moments wondering if he's happy, if he's lonely, and if he likes you. You hate yourself for this, but you can't help it—which is why the night Nibbles the hamster first escaped, I was frantic.

I was concerned about my ten tender digits, but more importantly, I worried about his welfare. He was so helpless, so tiny, and so fragile. I imagined him wandering aimlessly throughout the cold, damp, dark basement, dangers lurking in every corner and inside every box. To a hamster, a run-in with a plastic Easter bunny might be like coming face to face with King Kong; a run-in with a pointed Christmas star could be, well, deadly. Of course, I didn't share that kind of detailed information with my daughter, Lauren.

Equipped with flashlights and carrot sticks, Lauren and I searched every nook and cranny, calling in mournful cries, "Nibbles, Nibbles come home!" But to no avail. That night I couldn't sleep knowing one of the children was roaming the world alone, instead of being tucked safely beneath his pine shavings.

The next evening, growing tired of our glum faces, my husband, Tony, descended the basement stairs in search of Nibbles. He shouted up within seconds and announced, "I found him."

Lauren and I raced down the stairs to greet him, bearing the fatted calf of hamster food—every fresh fruit and vegetable we could find in the fridge.

First, as any good mother would do, I scolded him. "Nibbles, you ungrateful little fur ball! How could you do this to us? We fed you, gave you fresh water, and bought you this beautiful home in which we created a virtual ecosystem simulating your natural environment!"

"Is this the thanks we get?" added Lauren.

(I was impressed. Lauren showed true mother potential.)

"You scurry off without a care in the world and not even a squeak as to where you're hiding!" she continued.

Of course, like any ungrateful rug rat, Nibbles just gnawed on a carrot stick and ignored us.

"You know, it's weird," Tony said as Lauren continued scolding Nibbles. "It's almost as if he was waiting for me to find him."

"Don't be ridiculous," I said. "He's only a baby." But after the tenth time Nibbles escaped, and we scolded him and fed him fresh apple slices and cold, crisp lettuce leaves, I was beginning to see the picture.

"Mom, Nibbles is gone again." Lauren would mention non-chalantly while buttering her morning toast.

"How long has he been gone this time?"

"Two days."

"He'll be home soon," I assured her.

Thanks to Nibbles, I have a pretty good idea of what it will be like when my children leave the nest. One day, out of the blue, they'll begin to see the negative side of living in the lap of luxury and decide to break out on their own. They will tell me they want to make their own decisions, seek exciting adventures, and see the world. At first I'll worry that they might starve to death, so I'll lure them back with a home-cooked meal. And just like Nibbles, they'll stay long enough to fill their cheek pouches with life-sustaining nourishment, then venture out again.

After Lauren left for school, I opened the basement door to check the trap she'd concocted to catch Nibbles. And, sure enough, there he was, nestled in pine shavings. The trail of food Lauren had left leading to his home was all gone. One day my daughter is going to make a wonderful mother.

CHAMP GOES TO SCHOOL

One of the most engaging games I play with our adorable new puppy, is Fake Out Mommy So She Looks Like an Idiot.

Yes, it's nonstop, action-filled fun when cute, cuddly Champ gets a hold of a sock, pacifier, or the checkbook and gnaws on it as if it were his favorite chew toy. Mommy is under the delusion that simply telling Champ to "drop it" will result in him letting it go. But this only happens with dogs on television.

In real life, when Mommy needs check 234 for groceries, she makes a grab for it but Champ scampers off with the book behind the coffee table.

This is not a random choice on Champ's part, mind you. It's a cold, calculated move, employed so that either way Mommy moves, Champ can run in the opposite direction. And if she does manage to fake him out, which happens every fifty-sixth time, Champ casually saunters under the table and comes up staring at her as if she's some kind an idiot!

Of course, he'll only play this game when Mommy's home alone, because he knows with two people, he can easily be cornered. But with one stupid human, the game can go on—for hours and hours—until Mommy finally gives up, throws Champ a pen and lets him write the check for groceries. (And they say a dog never reaches beyond the intelligence level of your average two year old. Obviously, Buddy is the sole reason Clinton hung on to the presidency as long as he did.)

Another favorite pastime game is Wake Up Daddy at Three in the Morning and Pretend Like You've Really Gotta' Go, Until You Get Outside and Then Just Stand There and Enjoy the Early-Morning Breeze for the Next Half-Hour.

Our family soon realized that, although Champ has neglected to contribute one red cent to the mortgage, he thinks he owns the house.

According to some people who've never actually owned a dog, Champ needed to go to school. Personally, I felt school would only give Champ the opportunity to hang out with other dogs and brag about how they duped their stupid humans all day long:

"I had her behind the coffee table for six hours today."

"I grabbed his glasses off the counter. He couldn't even see me to catch me. Then I wore the glasses and read the stock page. I tried to tell him to buy Intel, but he just thought I was trying to tear up the paper."

I would've gladly suffered the humiliation if I could've put Champ on the school bus at 8 A.M. and welcomed him home in the late afternoon. But to my dismay, an adult is expected to accompany the pet to doggie school!

It was to be Champ and me, which gave a whole new meaning to the phrase, "yanking my chain."

The first night of class the whole family came along for support. The room was filled with yappers, sniffers, and slobberers in all shapes, colors, and sizes—and there were a lot of dogs there, too.

The instructor asked, "What's your dog's name?"

Our three-year-old Jenna piped up confidently, "Pain in the Butt!"

The class began with us stupid humans trying to control our dogs and listen to the instructor at the same time, which is like walking and chewing gum. Then a familiar but horrible odor wafted over the room.

"Ah, gee, who did it?" I said holding my nose.

"Champ did," the instructor informed me, while steering me toward the clean-up materials."

After some instruction, I discovered that dog trainers employ the same method of discipline used in child rearing: treats, or the more formal name: "What will you give me if I do what you want?" So, as long as I had hot dogs, Champ was an A+ student. But when they ran out, Champ was sent to the principal's office.

Once at home, we were to continue practicing the "praise, release, and reward" steps to proper behavior. If Champ refused to listen, I had some new techniques, too. I could spray him in the face with a water bottle or grab him by the scruff of the neck and tell him, "No" in a firm voice.

After three weeks of training, I must admit I'm thrilled with the results. My commitment to daily training has really paid off—not in Champ, of course. He still yanks my chain. But the kids are coming along nicely.

"Marcus, sit!"

"Jenna, stay!"

"Lauren, bring me the newspaper!"

"Good kids! Good kids!"

CHAMP GOES TO THE DOCTOR

If you're not a dog lover (and through no fault of your own—except for that one minor character flaw you possess of being born completely STUPID!), and you find that you now own a dog, I know a way you can instantly fall head over heels in "like" with your canine. Get him fixed.

We knew it was time to get Champ fixed when he started marking. Like most males, Champ became obsessed with leaving his imprint on everything: this tree, that bush, this table, that mail carrier, this computer, that red dress. I imagined him saying to himself, "Everything is mine! Mine! Mine!"—just like the Bills (Clinton and Gates).

So I called to set up the appointment.

The best part of the surgery was that Champ was gone all day. I could get some real work done in my office. I could finally write without stopping for anybody's scratching, whining, and frequent potty breaks except my own. Yup, just as soon as I got 3,000 points on Space Cadet Pinball, I would get to work.

Later that afternoon, I received a call saying the surgery was over and that I could bring Champ home because everything had gone well.

"Are you sure?" I asked with concern in my voice. "Don't you think you should keep him for another day? There might be complications."

"Mrs. DiSandro, you pull that every time Champ comes in to get his haircut. You need to come now."

Champ came out of the office, a little slower than usual. He glanced up at me. His face said it all: "How could you do this to me, you evil she-devil?"

My mother-guilt button was instantly activated. Then I saw the stitches. "Oh, my God, he has stitches!" I cried in horror.

"Of course," the vet said matter of factly, "that's how it's done."

"I didn't know my baby was going to suffer so," I said, scooping Champ up in my arms and carrying him to the car.

At home, Champ was not supposed to irritate the stitches, so the nurse suggested boxer shorts. We slipped on a pair of my son's plaid shorts and Champ waddled around the kitchen like a little man, scratching himself. (I'm not sure, but I think he wanted a beer.)

While recuperating, Champ behaved like a brave little patient. He'd sleep for hours and, to my dismay, hardly even coughed up a little bark. He was virtually speechless. So I interpreted for him: "You want me to warm your blankie for you, Champie? Here, mommy will put it in the dryer for you. Would you like some hot doggie, baby? Here, mommy will take the skin off so you don't choke."

But by the third day, something awful happened. I immediately phoned the vet. "Something is terribly wrong, Doc," I said, choking back tears. "Champ is tipping over the garbage can, chewing up shoes, puking up paper towels, and having accidents on the floor."

"Good, good." said the vet. "It sounds like our Champ is back to being a healthy puppy."

"No!" I protested. "Please, Doc," I begged. "Can I bring him in for another surgery?"

That's when *he* called me a sicko.

Animal activists, don't worry. I'm learning to love and accept Champ with all his little idiosyncrasies. Besides, he's the only one in the house I can beat at Space Cadet Pinball.

NIBBLES—GONE BUT NOT FORGOTTEN SOON ENOUGH

I thought you should know. Nibbles (sniff, sniff), Houdini of the Habitrail (sniff, sniff), died. I'll pause here to give you a moment to take it in.

Okay, that's long enough.

Just one month shy of his second "Gotcha Day" (the day my daughter personally selected him from a cage of like rodents), Nibbles (sob) the hamster (sob) has bit (sob) the big one.

Some may say, "Gone too soon," while others, like me, say, "Not soon enough." However cold-hearted that may sound, it is in no way meant to diminish the profound impact his short life had on so many.

Nibbles, better known as Nibs, helped us to look beyond our petty prejudices and strong aversions to small, gray mammals. And although some of us, like me, may never be able to fully embrace a member of the mouse family without shaking all over and shrieking, "GET THAT DISGUSTING THING AWAY FROM ME!" we are better for having known him. In his messy, smelly way, Nibs taught us important life lessons, many of which we will never forget, no matter how hard we try.

He taught us about gratitude. I'm grateful that my husband found him first. I always dreaded the day I would peer into the pine shavings and find Nibs stiffer than a Popsicle stick. Had the tragedy occurred when my husband was out of town, I would've been forced to beg, plead, and promise to wash my neighbor's car for a month before she'd agree to come over and properly dispose of him. Yes, I will always be eternally grateful for his well-timed demise.

Nibbles taught my daughter, Lauren, how to care for a living creature and, more importantly, how to blow-dry and style hamster fur. Yes, on occasion, when the distinct scent of hamster odor overwhelmed us, Nibs was washed, set, and styled. But Lauren was always careful to use a cool setting to avoid any unnecessary split ends.

Like Houdini, Nibbles was a legend in his own right. An expert escape artist, he astounded us with his genius and skill for breaking out of, and sometimes simply breaking, the many, many, homes we purchased for him. He taught us just how expensive one little brown bugger could be—condos, gourmet meals, pine shavings, toys, chew sticks, along with state-of-the-art exercise equipment. This may not be the most appropriate time to mention it, but that . . . that FUR BALL cost us well over three hundred bucks!

Of course, money is inconsequential when you think of the companionship such an animal brings to a family. Baby Jenna loved Nibbles. Although she often mistook him for a "goggy," or doggy, they often shared the same chew toys and the same toothbrush. (Lauren used it to shine Nibble's fur coat, but Jenna often found it lying around and used it to brush her own incoming teeth.)

Although he's been gone for more than a week, traces of his life still linger. His distinct scent will probably waft throughout our basement forever, negatively affecting the resale value of our home. Like Christmas tree needles, his pine shavings will continue to appear in the most unlikely places, like last night's chili con carne. And no matter how many times I vacuum, Jenna will manage to find a piece of hamster food (at least I hope it's the food) in the deep recesses of the carpet.

Yes, it's a difficult time for all of us. My daughter, Lauren, moped around the house, mourning his passing, crying, and sob-bing, on and on for oh, about . . . two seconds, before she said, "Can we get another one?"

To which I replied, "Well, dear, we need to wait the appropri-ate amount of grieving time before we can even consider such a notion—out of respect for (sob) Nibbles and all."

"How long will that be?" she asked.

"Let's see. How many years is it until you turn eighteen and can move out on your own?"

"Nine."

"That's exactly how long."

CHAPTER 6

Duels in a Duo

Marriage is the alliance of two people, one of whom never
remembers birthdays and the other who never forgets them.
—Ogden Nash

WOMEN ARE FROM THE BOUDOIR; MEN ARE FROM THE BASEMENT

My husband, Tony, and I were vacationing at home for a week.
And after only two days, we discovered that spending a vacation in
the comfort and coziness of our own home gives a busy husband
and wife the much-needed time to connect, relax, and hold meaningful conversations, while secretly plotting how to kill each other.

To my husband, a good vacation starts with a list. To me, it
starts with a nap.

I long to forget about cooking, cleaning, and column writing—to stop and smell the roses with the man I love. He wants
to—no, *needs* to—paint the window-well covers. And he desires
for the woman he loves to get lost!

"You're hovering again," my husband complains.

"I'm taking time to stop and inhale the paint fumes," I say,
dripping sarcasm.

"Very funny, Deb."

"But this doesn't *feel* like a vacation," I whine. (*Note:* All
woman whine on at-home vacations.)

"There you go with that feely stuff. What's a vacation supposed to *feel* like?"

"Like you're having fun! Like you've put aside your daily routines to relax and share in each other's company."

"Okay, okay, I hear you," he finally concedes. "Grab a paint brush. But don't leave any drips."

"Do you know you have an obsessive retentive personality?"

"Do you know you have an irritating way of moping around the house all morning that drives me absolutely crazy?"

"I'm depressed because I thought we were going to spend time together. I thought we were going to bond. I'll bet bonding never even crossed your mind," I said accusingly.

"Sure, it did," he said defensively. "I thought about it a lot. As a matter of fact, I'm going to bond that broken shelf in the basement as soon as I'm finished here."

Besides bonding, men also find at-home vacations the ideal time to take their perfectly running cars into the "shop" to have them "checked out." And while the car is at the "shop," they're checking out the nearest Home Depot, feverishly fingering shiny gadgets and doodads while grunting from the pure tool-time pleasure of it all.

I waited an entire afternoon for my husband to return so we could have lunch together. He bounced through the door at 5 P.M. and announced, "I bought something just for you, honey."

"You did? You thought about *me?*" I was ready to forgive him.

"Look. It's a dimmer switch for the laundry room," he oozed.

I was ready to kill him.

The dimmer switch became a sixteen-hour project that required turning off the power to the entire house sixty times, then resetting all the clocks and timers.

Of course, we did bond while grocery shopping together, a pastime I usually partake of alone, and now I know why. It's a wonder my cart ever made it to the checkout lane without the dairy products to the left, fresh produce to the right, canned goods on the bottom, and the milk and potatoes underneath! Our cart was arranged so beautifully that people often stopped to admire it.

At the checkout lane, my husband spent an hour showing the bagger how to properly bag our groceries. The manager offered him a job.

Back at home, he showed me how to properly put the groceries away. I offered to bounce a can of SpaghettiOs off his head.

Yes, at-home vacations bring out the many differences between men and women, which is why I recommend that all sharp objects be removed from the house before beginning one. As a matter of fact, I feel so strongly about this important issue, affecting the very lives of at-home vacationing couples everywhere, that I've decided to devote the rest of my vacation to writing a self-help book. The working title is *Women Are from the Boudoir; Men Are from the Basement.* And since I'm finding it difficult to concentrate with all the drilling and banging going on (I don't want to ask, but I believe my husband is installing a screwdriver organizer in the tool shed), I'm booking the next flight to Barbados.

ONCE UPON A BMW

Let's face it. After ten or fifteen years of marriage, you go through peaks and valleys. Some couples climb their way out. Others learn to live with a few lumps and bumps. And some unfortunate souls wind up with tremendous breakdown, a decline from which they never spring back.

But there's no need to suffer so miserably. With men and women living longer lives, why stick it out when it only makes us downright miserable. Right?

At least that's how I explained it to my husband. He didn't want to believe it at first. But once I pointed out all the apparent problems, he was, at least, willing to listen.

"I need more support," I explained as gently as possible. "I need more space, less pressure, and a better quality of life."

He stared at me in disbelief. "And you think a new mattress is gonna give you all that?!"

"Yes!" I exclaimed. "Our mattress has more lumps than your mother's mashed potatoes! I'm tossing and turning into the crannies and crevices so often during the night that I wake up seasick."

"Pills for motion sickness would be a lot cheaper. Besides," my loving husband added, "I don't have any problem sleeping on it."

"You could fall asleep in the middle of a monster-truck rally—while riding in the truck!" I reminded him.

"What's your point?" he asked.

"Honey," I explained with deep empathy, "I'm concerned about your health. Our mattress-edge breakdown is so bad that the other night you rolled right off and slept on the floor."

"I did?"

"No," I assured him, "but I'm almost certain that's what's gonna happen tonight." To my delight and surprise, we went mattress shopping.

We quickly realized mattresses had come a long way since we purchased our last set, which was thrown in free with our then-new bedroom furniture. A pocketbook of mattress translations might've helped.

As we wound our way through the mazes of mattresses, we learned about the various sleep systems, coil constructions, fibers baked in ovens, and beds designed by NASA. How that related to sleeping, we'll never know.

Mattresses start from your standard model all the way up to the "fully loaded," which has the same coil construction used on the Golden Gate Bridge.

The salesperson eagerly invited us to lie down. I felt embarrassed and gently sat on the edge, unlike my husband, who gladly fell onto the bed. He was suffering from sticker shock.

Attempting to explain the vast difference in prices, the salesperson said, "It's like comparing a Yugo to a BMW."

"I don't want to take it out on the highway," my husband barked. We laid down on the BMW as the salesperson fed us with tales of quality construction. My husband turned to whisper in my ear: "These coils are just a bunch of Slinkys tied together. I could build the box spring and save us a bundle."

I ignored my husband and sank into the luxurious comfort.

"So what do you think?" A voice boomed. I opened my eyes to find the salesperson towering over us. It suddenly occurred to me that when buying a mattress you are in one of the most vulnerable positions possible to make a sound purchase.

"We need to shop around," my husband said as we stood up to leave.

The salesperson followed us to the door. "Here's my card, my home phone number, a picture of my wife and six kids, and . . . did I forget to show you one of our finest used models?"

"Used models?" my husband eagerly asked.

"It's only been slept on by an eighty-pound woman from Pasadena. She had insomnia, so it's practically like brand new."

As we hurried to our car, he promised to wash our van if we came back.

In hopping from store to store and bed to bed, like Goldilocks, we discovered that no two stores sell the same exact mattress, so it's almost impossible to comparison shop. The designers have come up with 1,000 different ways to achieve the same result: a good night's sleep on a comfy bed. We were so confused we went home and took a nap.

After tossing and turning amid the peaks and valleys, we rushed back to the store and selected a BMW that would last us thirty years.

"Look at it this way," I said to my husband. "By the time this mattress is finished, we'll be in nursing-home beds."

"Nonsense!" my hubby protested, flexing his flabby muscles. "We'll be riding motorcycles across country well into our seventies."

"Forget the motorcycles." I suggested. "We'll just put wheels on our BMW."

IN SICKNESS AND IN FENDER BENDER

It was a paragon of perfection, a wild berry, streamlined vision of a vehicle at its best: tilt steering, power windows, power brakes, and, believe it or not, built-in drink holders.

My husband loved our new van more than, well, me.

"Don't be absurd," he'd say. "I love you, too, honey. Now, get out of the way so I can take a picture of our new baby." For three months, he extolled the virtues of van ownership to anyone who'd listen: "Plenty of room for the kids, and it's got a V-6 engine. I mean, this baby can RIP!"

"Rip?" I'd ask. "There will be no ripping around in this vehicle."

While my husband, Tony, praised and polished, I steered and feared our new vehicle. Sounds of screeching tires, fender benders, and soda stains on the plush, gray interior haunted my nightly dreams.

Tossing and turning, I'd wake up screaming, "Oh, no, it's a scratch on our new car. I've ruined it! I've ruined it!"

Tony comforted, and interrogated, me. "There, there, Deb. It's only a dream," he'd assure me while gently patting my back. "It better be a dream!" he'd say while running out to the garage with a floodlight and a magnifying glass.

Whenever I got behind the wheel, I drove just like the little old lady from Pasadena, only not as fast.

"Mom, are we there yet?" my children often complained. "We've been in the car for an hour and the park is only five minutes from our house."

"I'm searching for the perfect parking place," I'd explain. "And here it is!"

"We're in our garage," my son pointed out.

"That's right; everybody out. We can walk to the park."

When I was forced to actually park in public places, my three children got out and guided me into the spot with the same methods used to land a 747.

Then, after a month or two passed without mishap, I began to relax. The nightmares subsided, and at times, I even enjoyed driving our new van. By the third month, I was high on my own competence. Then one summer evening, it happened.

BAAAAM!

The van shook like a bowlful of wild-berry Jell-O.

"WHAT WAS THAT?" I cried, turning around.

It was a pole—a huge, black, cement pole. My fender was wrapped around it like a baby blanket.

"Oops," my front-seat passenger commented.

"It's okay," I assured my friend. "I've got a plan. I'll get out and stand in front of the van. When I say go, just step on the gas."

"But you'll be killed!" she gasped.

"Yes, but it will be quick," I explained. "And definitely less painful than telling my husband."

My sympathetic passenger patted my back. "There, there," she said, rubbing my trembling hand. "It'll be alright. In my twenty years of marriage, I've had a few fender benders myself. Here's what you do. Don't say anything."

"What do you mean don't say anything?"

"Maybe he won't notice."

"WON'T NOTICE! There are only two things my husband fondles when he gets home—checks in the mail and the van in the garage."

"Then say someone hit you in the parking lot."

Now, there was an idea, except I knew Tony wouldn't rest until the culprit was found and hung by her own jumper cables, and eventually, that would be me! For the rest of the dreaded ride home, my companion and I discussed our spouses' obsessions with dent-free cars.

"Why is it that we feel so guilty when we have an accident? I mean an accident is just that, an accident, right?" my friend lamented.

"Exactly," I agreed.

"Just because I dented a few doors, smashed a bunch of bumpers, and tore the side off my husband's Plymouth, does that make me a criminal?" she asked.

"You tore the entire side off . . ."

"I sideswiped a bus."

I had dinged a few doors in the past myself. And Tony's first response was always, "Just as long as you're all right." But somewhere around the third or fourth ding, he had stopped saying that. In fact, he stopped saying anything—for six days.

"Tony, darling," I called while crawling into the house. "Remember when we vowed to love each other in sickness and in health?"

"Yes," he said, eyeing me suspiciously.

"Well, I can assure you that although you feel healthy now, you're going to be sick." My husband flew out the side door and into the garage. All I heard was a pained gurgle escape from his mouth.

And then he said it, "Just as long . . . as you're all rrrrrright." Or was it, "Get me my jumper cables!"

It wasn't a good time to ask him to repeat it.

To make it easier to adhere to our wedding vows in the future, Tony's checking into a used car that I can drive without worry. He thinks he can pick up a Hummer from Desert Storm for a steal.

NEW STUDY LINKS BRAIN LOSS TO PHONE BILLS

I have discovered the key link to senility, for which I will one day be awarded the coveted Nobel Prize, or a gift certificate to Discovery Zone.

Based on sound scientific research, conducted at the Slightly Off Institute of Whining, I and my esteemed colleagues (a group of big complainers) learned that losing one's mind has absolutely nothing to do with age but is the direct result of years of reading one's phone bill.

We traced our findings all the way back to the first bill ever written when the caveman waved the sixty slabs of slate under his wife's nose and said, "Who the heck did you talk to in Poughkeepsie for seventy-two minutes?!"

The wife, wielding a granite spatula, kindly pointed out that it wasn't *her* fault the bill was so high, but the phone company's, with all their ridiculous charges and trumped-up calling plans, and that it was *his* fault for moving to a cave so far away from her friends and family.

And then, instead of shedding a few tears, which may have garnered her some sympathy, she lost her temper and resorted to name calling: "You . . . you neanderthal!" she cried.

To which the husband replied, "That's it, I'm ripping this phone off the wall!"

To which the wife replied, "Oh yeah? Will that be before or after I rip the hair you have left off your head?"

"What could you possibly have to say to your friend for four thousand, three hundred and twenty seconds?" he asked in exasperation.

"Things!" she said defensively.

"Things?" he shot back. "I talked to my friend Tim the other night for fifteen minutes and we had 'things' wrapped up in five minutes. The rest of the time we talked about subwoofers."

"What does your friend care about what kind of dog we get?"

The husband shook his head. "It's a bass enhancer for the surround-sound stereo system."

"And you wasted your call talking about that?!"

Tsk. Tsk. Had they only been born a billion years later, they could've read *Men Are from Mars, Women Are from Venus* and realized that wives use the phone to communicate, while men use it to order seventy-six-dollar never-need-sharpening ninja knife sets off the Home Shopping Network.

Finally, after much introspection, and because her kids said she had to, the wife decided to seek out the best calling plan. To restore peace to the "cavedom," she vowed to cut the phone bill in half.

First, she analyzed the bill itself, which cost her six billion brain cells right there, and discovered that without even dialing, the local bill—with its federal and state taxes, infrastructure maintenance fee, access charge, feature-usage charge, mandatory charge, and just-because-we-can charge—was already forty bucks!

The operator then informed her that for interstate, intrastate, and international calls, she would need to pick another carrier.

"What about intercosmic and interplanetary calls?" the wife sarcastically inquired.

The operator did not share her sense of humor. Click.

The first month, she tried the 10-10 numbers (where you pay as little as ten, or even five, cents a minute), but she soon learned that those deals only apply if you call for exactly twenty-four minutes and thirty-six seconds between the hours of 3 and 4 A.M. every other leap year. And if you sneeze during the call, it's an extra ten cents.

She searched the Internet, filled out dozens of surveys to find the best long-distance plan to fit her needs, and learned that she was too needy. She learned that "slamming" is not what you do with the phone when a telemarketer calls, and "cramming" is not what you do when you cram the bill into your purse so your husband doesn't see it. But "bamming" is what you do with your head and a wall when you finally realize that the only way to cut the phone bill in half is to use scissors.

The husband came home after a long day of talking to his

fellow hunters about subwoofers and found his wife curled up in the corner, mumbling incoherently.

He looked around the cave and said, "What did you do all day?"

She had no choice but to rip the remaining hair off his head. She pleaded insanity on *Cave Court TV.*

DO YOU PROMISE TO LOVE, HONOR, AND KEEP YOUR MITTS OFF THE THERMOSTAT?

Many hundreds of years ago, when my husband and I first considered tying the noose—uh, I mean, knot (ha-ha, just a little marriage humor there)—we felt confident that ours would make for a happy union. We shared the same values, religion, and deep-seated love for buttered popcorn.

But to ensure our success, and because Father Henry said we had to, we attended a pre-wedding weekend at our church. Again, we discovered that we wholeheartedly agreed on other potential marital problems like money, kids, and the placement of toilet-seat lids.

But after seventeen years of thermostrife, it seems the church and other experts failed to tell us the truth. That marriage is like a faucet. When one gets hot, the other is cold. When one gets cold, the other is hot.

Along with the mandatory blood test, every engaged couple should be required to take a thermostat test, in which they're both locked in a room with nothing between them but a thermostat control. There, they'll learn how long they can coexist before one of them kicks down the door shouting, "I can't take it anymore; this nut thinks normal is ninety-two degrees!"

I am quite serious here. Because, without this testy temperature test, differences are bound to have an adverse affect on your marriage, the electric bill, and the meter reader—if your husband chases him out of the backyard with a rake, shouting, "You lie! There's no way our reading could be that high!"

This past summer our thermostat experienced more ups and downs than a manic-depressive on a roller coaster.

"One minute you're hot; the next, you're cold," my husband nagged.

"Oh yeah?" I accused him. "First, you turn it on, then you turn it off."

"And what about you?" He retaliated. "I turn it down; you turn it up! I turn it up; you turn it down."

My husband desires the temperature in our house at a comfortable seventy-eight degrees. I find seventy-four more to my liking, with a cool seventy-two ideal for a perfect night's slumber.

"I'm hot!" I complain while trying to sleep on a sultry summer evening.

"Take the covers off," he suggests.

"But I can't sleep without covers."

"Why?"

"Because I'll get cold."

Once he's sleeping peacefully, I sneak downstairs and turn down the thermostat.

Within a half-hour, he sits straight up and says, "I can hear the dial on the meter twirling. I'm turning it up."

At night, we listen to the weather report with rapt attention. My husband longs to turn the air conditioning off.

"It'll be seventy tonight," he rejoices. "We can turn it off."

"But it's going back up to ninety tomorrow," I explain. "Just leave it on. It'll cost more if you turn it on and off."

"That's just an old wives' tale."

"Is not."

"Is too!"

"No way!"

"Way!"

I called the electric company to get some answers. The first customer-service guy said seventy degrees is the average thermostat temperature, give or take a few degrees, in most houses. Then he gave me another number. The environmentally obnoxious guy at the Nature First Program said seventy-eight was the best place to leave the thermostat. When I told him I like to turn it down to seventy-two at night, he reached through the phone and slapped me.

Of course, in the winter, it's the opposite. My husband walks around in shorts, while his breath freezes in midair. I sneak over to the thermostat in my six layers of thermal wear and push it up to eighty. He saunters by later in his bathing trunks and notches it down to seventy.

I asked my husband what the thermoatmosphere was like in his house when he was a child.

"My parents always played Russian roulette with the dial," he admitted.

"Ah hah!" I said triumphantly.

"I always thought my dad was environmentally ahead of his time," my husband continued. "But now I know the truth."

"What's that?" I asked, hoping for some profound wisdom passed on from a man married forty years.

"He was just cheap."

PERSONALITIES PUCKER IN THE PAINT

What happens when a wonderfully creative, right-brained person marries a logical, left-brained bozo, I mean person? At some point, they end up having a showdown in the middle of the paint aisle at Menards.

Rows of satin finish and semigloss stand at attention as twenty couples, pretending not to notice, watch on the sidelines.

The enemies face each other, deadly weapons drawn: his, a 1¼-inch paintbrush, hers, a revolutionary faux finishing tool.

The paint cans tremble.

"Why can't we just paint the walls with a brush like everybody else does?" he asks, waving the bristles in her face.

"A paintbrush? Why a paintbrush when this wool sponge can marble, stripe, and color wash?" she replies, swatting near his nose with the woolly turned weapon.

"Because it's the dining room, Deb. People want to eat in there, not be sick."

A gasp is heard from the onlookers.

"Are you saying my decorative walls make people sick?"

"Well, whenever I come out of our multistriped, marbleized, stuccoed, veined bathroom, I have a headache."

She withdraws her weapon and walks dejectedly back to the faux finishing aisle.

He hears sniffling. "Now don't start to make a scene. You know I hate to make a scene. Okay, okay," he says, reluctantly returning the paintbrush to the hook. "You can woolly, or whatever it's called."

She smiles in victory.

"But I get to pick the color."

POW! She's been shot!

"What? What?!" she cries.

"Now here's a color I can live with," he says, pulling a paint sample from the display case."

"That's not a color. It's Off-White."

"It's a great color. It's clean—"

"It's boring. I was thinking more of a *Rouge Framboise*."

"Sounds like a new strain of flu."

"It's the shade between Royal Renaissance and Grape Fizz."

"You want to gripple our dining room in Grape Nehi?"

"The technique is called stipple," she corrected him.

"Gripple, stipple, shmipple. I can't eat in a purple room."

"It's more of a mauve."

"Oh, well then, okay!" He says sarcastically, flinging a gallon of tint base toward the innocent clerk.

"Honey," she says rubbing his arm with the wool sponge. "You know painting nurtures my creative side."

"Why does your creative side have to be so . . . so . . . off the wall?"

"Very funny."

"I like my walls to be neat and tidy and—"

"Perfect? Is that what you're saying? I bet when you were a kid you lined up your toys in perfect little rows."

"And by color, too," he added. "The blue trucks first, then the yellow tractors next . . ."

"I'll tell you what," she suggests. "If you let me pick the color, I'll let you hang the pictures back up any way you want."

"Really?"

"You can use your level and everything."

"All right! And will you promise not to use my clam knife to open the paint can?"

"Maybe."

The paint clerk sighs with relief. "It looks like a draw," he says. "Unfortunately, we weren't so lucky with the last couple. What a tragedy," he said shaking his head. "It was splattered everywhere."

"What was splattered everywhere?" we asked.

"Turquoise-Mocha Delight and Off-White."

SING US A SONG, YOU'RE THE GADGET MAN

Whenever I hear Billy Joel's "Piano Man" on the radio, I'm reminded of my dear, helpful husband. No, he's not the Piano Man, he's the Gadget Man.

Thanks to him, I have more kitchen gadgets than Julia Child. And although he's never actually cooked an entire meal in our kitchen, my husband believes it's his mission to make me a more efficient cook. To show my heartfelt appreciation for his ongoing support, I plan to take his nose and wind it through the Popeel pocket garlic press he gave me for Christmas! Or maybe I could use the salad spinner he gave me for Easter?

Did you know that it's labor intensive to simply wash your lettuce, shake off the excess water, and put it in a bowl? According to my husband, the Gadget Man, in order to achieve maximum nonwilting proficiency, I need to wash the lettuce, then feel my way through the maze of handy gadgets in the pantry, locate the three parts of the salad spinner, put them together, tear the lettuce, toss it into the spinner, turn the handle approximately 16,003 times, and then toss the lettuce into the salad bowl.

Do you want to keep your buns warm? There is no substitute for a microwave bun warmer. Of course, first you must locate the microwave pad and the special napkin that fits into the pad and the basket, and you'll have warm buns throughout your leisure dinner. Except in our family, the kids usually finish the rolls before I can scrape them off the baking pan.

Of course, no kitchen would be complete without the Happi-Helper Gadget Man ordered from a catalog. The Happi-Helper not only chops, whips, and mixes, but also scrapes paint off your walls!

Who can forget the ninja knife set, able to cut through a tin can, that he ordered from television? Not me, because he never fails to demonstrate it to our dinner guests.

As any chef knows, you can't cook without the proper lighting. So my husband installed under-the-cabinet and over-the-counter-and-up lighting throughout the entire cooking preparation area. The glare glinting off the pot roast is so intense I have to wear shades. Okay, I'm kidding. But I'm not kidding about the colander tuna press. It's a tiny colander that fits over the opened tuna can so that you can drain the juice. (Don't be jealous. You can have one. We have two.)

Once, he came home and found me twirling around the kitchen with a head of lettuce in my hands.

"What are you doing?" he asked as drips of water slapped him in the face.

"I'm drying the lettuce!" I barked. "Your efficiency is killing me! Now, I think I've got vertigo."

"You're not supposed to twirl," he informed me. "Just the salad spins."

"Yeah, but I can't crank the spinner handle because of the carpal tunnel syndrome I've developed from winding the cheese into a fine powder with that superefficient hand-held cheese grater."

"Oh, sure," he smirked. "Next you're going to blame my efficiency for those pimples breaking out all over your forehead."

"Well, you're the one who bought that pitch fork," I reminded him.

"It's a barbecue fork," he snarled.

"I thought it was a multipurpose tool. You could easily use it during bow-hunting season to spear deer."

"Very funny, Deb. The fork didn't fit in the drawer so I hung it from the ceiling in the pantry. What does that have to do with your forehead?"

"These aren't pimples; they're prong marks! Every time I go in there, I bang into it."

That night, we ate dinner in silence. All you could hear was the hum from the dimmer switch that lit the kitchen table into the perfect dining mood. That is, until I started singing:

"Sing us a song, you're the Gadget Man. Buy us a gadget tonight. One that slices red beats and minces your meat and makes a great pick for your nose. Oh, la, la, la, la, la."

(I knew I'd sleeping on the couch that night, but it was worth it.)

COMMITTED TO MARRIAGE

What is it with all these single people taking a vow to never marry? They'll live together, hang out, or just plain date, but marriage is not in their vocabularies.

It's wrong I tell you. Wrong! Marriage is a covenant of give and take, love, and respect—the kind of togetherness that will put you right into an *institution*! Wait a minute. What I meant to say is that marriage is an institution and two people willingly entering into it should be *committed*!

Anyway, it is my duty as a happily married person to help these stray couples find their way to wedded blisters. I mean, bliss. Together married people can make a difference, one couple at a time. I'm starting with my husband's best friend, Tim.

Tim called the other day to talk to my husband about cars, jobs, and subwoofers. But before I handed over the phone, I casually asked about the girl he'd been dating for two years.

"So whaddya think? Is she the one?" I hedged.

"Yeah, she's great. Everything is great," he replied. It was the ideal opening for the question my husband refused to propose.

Of course, I had no trouble proposing, just ask my hubby. "Sooooo," I hinted. "Do I hear wedding bells?"

"No," he said firmly. "Why mess with something so perfect?"

"Because!" I said with exasperation. "That's what marriage is all about."

"You have a new dress to wear, right?" he guessed.

"Black with silver straps."

"Why don't you have your husband take you out to dinner?" he suggested.

"I believe there's a strict dress code at McDonald's," I explained.

"Did I mention we just came back from Paris?" Tim asked.

"Aha!" I shouted. "There, see, Paris. If you were married, you wouldn't have to waste your time in Paris when Niagara Falls is so much cheaper."

"My girlfriend paid for her own ticket. Besides," he added, "we don't need a piece of paper to prove our love for each other."

"Hold on a minute!" I coughed. "I'm choking here! A piece of paper?? You think that thing tossed in the bottom of the box marked Miscellaneous in my basement is just a piece paper?"

"We're happy this way," he insisted.

"Happy?" I guffawed. "You think you're happy? According to a new national survey, married people are mentally healthier than single people." (Suddenly, I felt someone nudging me. I turned to see my husband doubled over in laughter. "Be quiet!" I whispered. "You're diminishing my argument.") "The expert says," I continued, "that after five years of marriage your depression will be at it's lowest."

"But I'm not depressed," he said.

"Of course, you're depressed," I assured him. "You and your girlfriend are just too busy riding around on matching motorcycles and flitting off to Paris to notice!"

"We're as committed as any married couple," he stressed.

"You can't be committed, unless you're married," I assured him.

"Huh?"

"I can read your relationship like a book. You each have your own place, right?"

"Right."

"You always take a shower before you see each other."

"Of course."

"You treat each other like best friends."

"We do."

"And you're always considerate of each others feeeeelings."

"That's right."

"Well geeeeeee!" I shot back. "Anybody can stay together on those terms. You know what real love is? Married love? It's when your spouse sees you at your crabbiest, ugliest, smelliest self and still stands by you—although not too close. It's when you trust each other enough to call it "our" money, "our" bills, "our" problems. It's when you can finish each other's sentences and unspoken thoughts. It's when you admit your relationship isn't perfect. But you work at it, work at it, and work at it. It's the kind of partnership that makes you kinder, stronger, and braver. As Leland Foster Wood once said, "Success in marriage is much more than a matter of finding the right person; it is also a matter of being the right person." I paused to let my words sink in. Then I spoke. "So do you have anything to say?"

"Yeah, sure," he said. "Ask your husband what he thinks of those new PT Cruisers?"

I handed the phone to my husband and whispered. "I think he's softening. I can tell."

CHAPTER 7

Tackles the Teenage Years

You know your children are growing up when they stop asking
you where they came from and refuse to tell you where they
are going.   —P. J. O'Rourke

YIPPEE! WE HAVE A TEENAGER!

My son is on the threshold of becoming a teenager, a fact that
I'm really excited about because I recently discovered what has
to be the absolutely best part about having a teenager. I made
this discovery by accident, while we were bowling. Now, as
everyone knows, bowling is a fun family activity in which you
spend about three hours trying on somebody else's shoes and
approximately three minutes actually bowling.

It was while throwing my ball down the lane that this revelation about teens occurred. My ball was rolling toward the left
gutter rather quickly and I had to do something fast. Being a
savvy bowler, I knew that in order to get my ball to change
directions I had to frantically wave my arms to the right while
jerking my hip and head in the same direction and shout,
"This way! This way!" (Any semiprofessional bowler knows
that this encourages the ball to move back toward the middle
of the lane where it belongs, so that you can get a strike and
beat your husband.)

I was functioning in full bowler form, when I heard this piti-
ful wail from our table. I turned around just as I heard my ball

bounce into the gutter to see my twelve-year-old son, red-faced and seemingly melting into the bowling-alley floor.

"What happened?" I asked him. "Are you feeling okay?"

"Don't talk to me," he mumbled.

"What? What??"

"Shhh, somebody may think we're together."

"But we *are* together." I turned to my husband who was laughing into his bowling shoes. "What's wrong with him?"

"He's embarrassed," he explained.

"Embarrassed by what?" I asked.

"You?"

"Me?"

"The way you bowled."

"You're kidding," I said.

"Would you guys just stop talking, PLEASE!" My son begged while peeking out of the corner of his shirt, which he pulled up to his eyes.

My husband was up next. He winked at me, then walked to the line all dorkylike, which, unfortunately, wasn't hard for him to pull off.

My son was mortified. He spent the rest of the frame in the men's room.

My husband and I were having the time of our lives.

Hip, hip hooray! Our son finds us embarrassing!

We tried to control ourselves, really, especially after our son pretended he was with the family on the other side of the bowling alley.

But when you discover something this wonderful about parenting, you can't help but overdo it at first, which explains why, the other day, I burst out singing, "The hills are alive with the sound of music!" right in the middle of Kmart. My son wouldn't stop begging for one of those CDs with foul language and I realized that my out-of-tune song said so much more than a mere chastising ever could.

Now, when I want him to take out the garbage and he complains, I simply say, "Oh that's okay. I'll just slip on my pink pig slippers, this ratty, red bathrobe with the hole in the armpit, and let's see . . . your bike helmet and take out the trash all by myself. Hey, isn't that your girlfriend across the street?"

"NO WAIT!" he gasps, diving for the bag. "I'll do it. You just stay inside and shut the drapes, PLEASE!"

The scenarios are endless.

"Body piercing?"

"Sure, son! I'll go with you. You can get one in your ear; I'll get one in my bellybutton, and then I can wear one of those short tops like your girlfriend wears. Do you think these stretch marks will detract from the effect?"

"So you want to have some friends over? I hope you don't mind if I just mess up a bit. I want the house to have that same overall-disaster look that your bedroom has going on."

"Why don't I just come to school and pick up your homework, since you keep forgetting to bring it home. Just let me get my robe!"

A TOUR OF THE TEEN BRAIN

Today we're going to go inside the teen brain in an attempt to try to understand the intricacies of their complex thought processes. (Okay, I know nobody has that kind of time, but we'll at least skim the surface.)

Here we are inside the three-pound blob of gray matter known as the teenage brain. As you can see, it's quite spacious and airy, which is the explanation behind the well-known term "airhead."

This large mass here on the right, is the, uh, filamentous system. Yeah, that's right, fila-a-a-mentous. It alone is solely responsible for the teen's total preoccupation and obsession with filaments and explains why, if your house is on fire, your teen will stop in the bathroom and fix his hair before he would even consider jumping out a window to safety. (*Please note: Fixing the hair does not necessarily mean combing it, but messing it up to a perfect "just got out of bed" look that takes hours in front of the mirror to accomplish.*)

You will notice here on the left wall a neural circuitry that looks very much like a neon sign. As you can see, it blinks on and off, like a hotel-vacancy sign. That's exactly what it is! Now, you can understand why a teen could be in the same room with you and have no idea what's going on. Vacancy, no vacancy, vacancy, no vacancy. You never know when it will switch.

Over here, on the back wall is a shower nozzle. As you will observe, the nozzle is running at all times. It *never* switches off, explaining why a teen can jump in the shower at 6 A.M. and manage to stay in long enough to empty the town water tower. The circuitry that connects the amount of water used in the shower to the amount on the water bill won't be forged for years to come.

Let's walk to the front of the brain, commonly known as the prefrontal cortex. Unlike the adult brain, the teen's cortex is pierced with a ring. No big surprise there. But if you look closely, you will recognize it as one of those familiar mood rings. See how quickly it changes colors? This explains why one minute your teen can be telling you he's too mature to pick out pumpkins at the pumpkin farm and the next he's bawling like a baby because he didn't carve the eyes right on his Mr. Pumpky.

Over here, in the middle, is the massive and all-consuming Stupid System. Take, for instance, a teen having trouble in math. You can be certain that the teen will not, under any circumstances, go to the math lab, where there are dozens of teachers waiting to help him! Why? Because, as the teen explains, "I DON'T WANT TO LOOK STUPID!" Instead, the teen will ask his or her parents for help, so that when all the answers are wrong, you, the parent, will ultimately wind up looking the most stupid of all!

Not looking stupid is paramount to a teen. This is the reason why, when your teen comes home from a school dance, you never ask if they actually danced with anybody, because that would be stupid. Everybody knows teens *never* dance at dances, unless, of course, they've been seeing someone seriously for a long, long time—like say, from first-period math class through seventh-period science.

Stupidity also gives reason to the puzzling phenomenon known as e-mail. A teen must rush home and e-mail his friend, even if he lives next door, because it would be like soooo stupid to, like, just go up and ring his doorbell. Duh! Just like it would be stupid to expect your teen to attend Sunday Mass with a big zit in the middle of his forehead! You know everyone in the entire church would be staring directly at him instead of paying attention to the Mass.

It's not surprising that, with all this circuitry going on inside a teen's brain, they might be hearing voices, which is why they play their music as loud as the sound of a jackhammer ripping through concrete. It's their feeble attempt to blot out the voices.

Well, that's all we have time for today, folks. Now that you have some new information into your teen's psyche, remember to be patient. It won't be long before their big blob of gray forms into a perfectly hardheaded, boring, brainy mass like yours.

MEET "EVERYBODY ELSE"

My teenage son has made a new friend at school named Everybody Else. I haven't had the pleasure of meeting Everybody Else yet, but I've heard a lot about the kid.

When my son served detention for talking during class, he informed me, "Come on, Mom. It's no big deal. Everybody Else has, like, twenty detentions."

Everybody Else must have incredibly understanding parents, I thought.

One morning, I handed my son his lunch in a paper bag.

He smirked and said, "Everybody Else gets to buy lunch."

Everybody Else must be rich, I assumed.

It seems that Everybody Else must also be a genius, because, according to my son, the kid can spend hours on school nights playing computer games, e-mailing friends, and watching television and still manage to pull off straight As.

My son feels he should be able to stay up later than his younger siblings because he's "Not a Kid Anymore." And besides, Everybody Else gets to stay up way past ten o'clock.

Everybody Else must have the stamina of a star athlete, because if Not a Kid Anymore stays up past ten, he sleeps through his alarm, misses the bus, and Not a Kid Anymore's mom has to drive him to school!

On weekends, when I remind my son that he can't go out until his chores are done, he pouts and says, "Everybody Else doesn't have to help with chores."

Everybody Else must have a maid, I imagine.

Everybody Else also has a girlfriend, watches R-rated movies, plays violent video games, and hangs out at the mall for hours.

Frankly, Everybody Else is getting on my nerves. The kid's sneaky. Although I've asked my son to invite Everybody Else for dinner, the kid never shows up. When I ask him to get Everybody Else's parents on the phone so we can chat, they're never home.

At school events, I randomly point to somebody in big pants and ask my son, "Is that Everybody Else?"

He says, "No, that kid's parents are really strict. He has to do homework every night."

I point to a kid bouncing off the gym walls. "Is that Everybody Else? I'd really like to meet this character."

"Nope," Not a Kid Anymore says, "his parents have to approve every video or CD he buys."

So I seek out other parents and ask, "Do you have a son or daughter named Everybody Else?"

They say, "No but we've heard so much about the kid, we're starting a petition to get Everybody Else kicked out of school."

I signed it. My husband signed it. Even the dog, Champ, signed it. (It seems Everybody Else never has to walk the dog or pick up a pooper-scooper.)

One week, Everybody Else was going to miss a cross-country meet to go to a party. My son wanted to do the same.

I smiled as lovingly as I could and said to Not a Kid Anymore, "Thank goodness I don't have to see that Everybody Else grows up to be a kind, caring, responsible adult—just you. Now go get your track shoes."

RECORD PLAYERS ARE BACK AND PHAT

If you want to see your business flourish in these tumultuous times, just market your product to a teenager. It doesn't even have to be a new product. Just bring back some old, obsolete thing that the teenyboppers have never seen before, and they'll think it's "off the hook, fo' sho.'" (Translation: "Really neato mosquito!")

I recently made this economic discovery when my teenage son started asking for something called a Funkmaster Flex Package.

"Listen," I said, "none of those muscle-building gimmicks ever work. If you want to really flex your funk, take those hefty garbage cans out to the curb."

"Mom," he explained, pulling his pants up. (My son is forever pulling up his pants. When big pants go out of style, I worry about what he'll do with his hands.) "It comes with a high-performance mixer."

"Oh," I nodded in understanding, "that's no problem. We've got a high-performance Hamilton Beach mixer in the kitchen, third cabinet on the left."

My son shoved the newspaper ad under my nose. "This is a mixer," he said, "and the rest of the DJ set."

I stared at the picture. "This?" I asked in confusion. "This thing, here? But this is a . . . a . . . record player."

"A what?" my son asked.

"A record player. You know, before CDs, before cassettes, before eight-track tapes there were record players—phonographs."

"That's whack!" he laughed. (Translation: "That is so ridiculous!")

"These are called turntables," he explained. "And they come with this phat mixer, slipmats, an antiskate correction system, a strobe illuminator, and removable head shells!"

"You're not buying anything that requires you to wear a head shell!" I warned.

After an exhaustive on-line search and an enlightening visit to the music store, I learned that my son wanted to buy two record players so he could mix music together and then scratch it. (I also learned that a head shell is just a new name for the dust cover that fits over the record player.)

"So let me get this straight," I asked, trying to comprehend this new-old product. "You want to buy these two record players and a bunch of brand-new records so you can scratch them—on purpose?"

"Now you're down with it!" my son said.

"I'm down with what?" I asked. "I do have the sniffles. Maybe I'm coming down with a cold." My kid was too busy counting out his birthday and Christmas money to bother explaining that "down with it" meant "mommy, you're really hip!"

This is what happens after you've attempted to have a serious talk with your teenager. You logically explain to him why he needs something to occupy his free time other than television and computer games, and he goes out and chooses the most obnoxious, totally whack, illogical hobby he could find.

Well, at least we knew where he'd be at eleven o'clock at night.

I didn't see much of my son during holiday break. But I could hear him—scratching and mixing music produced by guys with big pants and chains that doubled as jewelry and twenty-inch rims on their 64 Impalas. Every few days, I'd pop in a couple of earplugs, go up to his room, and check to see if he was okay.

"Did you hear that?" he'd ask bopping his head so hard I feared it might fall off. "That was off the hook, dog!"

"Are you calling me a frog!" I gasped.

My son pulled out my earplugs and said, smiling, "Not a frog, mom, a dog."

"You called me a dog?!"

"Not just any dog," he assured me with a hug, "you're a phat dog!" (Translation: I'm not sure, but, hey, he hugged me. Of course, I had to hold his pants up.)

TEENAGE MUMBLE

My teenage son called an office-supply store to ask if they had a certain item in stock. I overheard his side of the conversation and could easily imagine the poor sales clerk's reply:

Teen: "Do you mumblemumblemumble?"

Store Clerk: "What did you say?"

Teen: (without changing tone or amount mumbling) "Do you mumblemumblemumble?"

Store Clerk: "WHAT???!!"

Teen: (sighing deeply) ". . . know (pause) stuff (long pause) write on (longer pause) post mumblemumble . . ."

Store Clerk: "Did I hear you say *poster?*"

Teen: "Yeah."

Store Clerk: "Poster board? Are you looking for poster board?" he shouted excitedly.

Teen: "Yeah."

Store Clerk: (wiping sweat from his brow) "YES, YES, we have poster board!"

Teen: "K, tha."

I'm not sure when it began. But my son's articulate and enthusiastic voice has gradually deteriorated into an unintelligible, monotone mumble. And it's continuing downward toward a grunt, a snort, and sometimes an almost imperceptible nod of the head as his only way of communicating with the outside world.

Now if I could figure out what the heck he was *saying,* I could hire myself out as an interpreter for teenagers and make millions!

Of course, it doesn't help matters that most teens are fascinated with their shoes, or maybe their teen brains are just too heavy to hold up, because they're always looking down and talking to the ground. This makes it difficult to find out their plans for the day.

I've discovered the best way to make eye contact and hold a meaningful conversation with my teen is to flop face first onto his big shoes with a Twix bar in one hand and a Mountain Dew in the other. (**Warning:** Make sure teen is not on skateboard at the time, or you could wind up between an ollie and a minivan.

"So, Marcus," I ask. "What's the plan for today?"

"Mumblemumblenothinmumble."

"No plans?"

"Ye."

"Would you like to go to the pool with your sisters?"

No reply.

"Was that a breeze blowing a strand of your hair, or did you kind of nod your head?" I ask.

"Mumblemumblehead!"

"Okay, we're leaving in ten minutes," I say, rolling off his shoes.

After church one Sunday, my son completely ignored his friend, Bert, while we stood talking to Bert's parents. I called him on it afterward and he claims he did talk to Bert.

"I didn't see you wave or even grunt," I confronted him.

"Did too. We talked 'bout skateboarding later."

"I didn't see you move a muscle!" I said, amazed that they could have held an actual conversation.

"Gosh, mom. Like, I'm not gonna get all excited and start yelling like you do. That's broke!"

"What's broke?"

"Talking."

"Talking is broke?"

"Yeah. I just lifted my left eyebrow. That's how I asked him if he wanted to skate. He said he'd call me later."

"And how did he answer you back without moving?" I asked in fascination.

"He lifted the top half of his left index finger."

Gee, well that explains it!

I see a new survivor show in the making. The object of the game is for adults to stay in the same room with a group of teenagers for as long as they can stand it. Whoever can decipher what they are saying is the winner. And the winner gets my teenager for a week!

A PBJ WRAPPER RAPS ON SON

As a parent, the significant moment when your sweet, helpless baby grows into a self-reliant, mature, responsible young person and first reveals his career aspiration is one you'll never forget.

"I want to be a rapper," my high-school freshman announced while hiking up his pants. My son spends twenty-three hours a day hiking, pulling—and when he runs, holding—up his pants because of one fact that somehow seems to escape his comprehension—they are too big for him!

Now all the parenting experts tell you this is not the time to

criticize your child's career choice. Instead, you should be supportive and encouraging. (Yeah, well that's because their kids
wanted to be lawyers and doctors, not wrappers!)

"So you want to be a wrapper." I repeated back. "Exactly what
are you going to wrap?" I asked in exasperation. "Wrapping presents at the mall isn't going to build you that house you always
talk about with the professional-sized basketball court and sixty-
seat movie theater, you know."

"Not a *wrapper*, mom," my astute teen explained, "a *rapper*,
like Tupac and Eminem and Snoop and Eazy E."

"I seesy E." I said.

"I want to get down and rap about my life and my homies."

"But most of those rappers get their inspiration from their
rough-and-tough childhoods, right?" I reminded him.

"Right."

"They've lived in dangerous neighborhoods and rap about the
hardships in their world. You've had a cushiony childhood compared to these guys. What are you gonna rap about, strife in the
suburbs?" I chuckled. Then, without warning, the chuckle
became a laugh, and the laugh became a guffaw, and suddenly—
after all those painstaking hours of listening to annoying,
rhyming, rapping sounds blasting on the car radio and booming
behind the bedroom door—I lost my grip.

"What would you call yourself?" I goaded him. "Hey, I got it.
The PBJ Rapper. Get it? Peanut Butter and Jelly *rapper*? Ooh,
that's good. Then I started slapping my hand against my thigh
and making those weird noises with my mouth, my hands flying
all over like the hands of the kids in the MTV videos. I grabbed
my vegetable brush for a microphone and before I could stop
myself, I was rapping.

"This is PBJ and I'm here to tell you/there's strife in the suburbs./It can get to you too./Can you picture my fate?/Eatin' vegeta-
bles I hate,/never stayin' up late./Takin' out garbage, cleanin' the
garage,/walkin' the dog./I got so many chores, my head's in a fog./

"TV in my room's got poor reception,/been beggin' the Ps for
a cable connection./There's no question, I'm stressin'./I be

moanin', groanin', snow blowin', lawn mowin',/that's where all my precious time's goin'.

"These burbs are full of strife./It's messin' with my life!/School might be cool, if there weren't so many tests,/and teachers weren't pests,/and we could rest on our desk./Homework's got to go./I already know what I need to know./So keep it slow.

"I got twenty-inch rims on my bike,/waitin' for driver's ed is some waitin' I don't like./Me and my homies chillin' at the mall,/I feel like dyin' when my mom starts to call,/ 'Marcus it's time to go!'/I'm mortified, gotta hide./She's ruinin' my reputation and causin' me constipation./I shout, spout, pout./When I'm eighteen, I'm movin' out./I be makin' my own route to the city,/where I'll be sittin' pretty,/far away from the strife in this suburban life."

I wrapped up my rap and looked around for my son. "Marcus? Wasn't that great? This gig isn't so bad after all. Hey, maybe we could rap together, you know, PBJ and M-O-M. We could go on tour with the M&Ms! Marcus?"

"My son is probably cryin',/but his tears he'll soon be dryin',/lookin' for a new career no doubt./See how it all works out!"

HE COULD'VE DANCED ALL NIGHT

As a dedicated, involved, and caring parent, early in the school year, I pledged to do my part for education. I eagerly signed up for the easiest volunteering duty before all the other parents beat me to it.

When a volunteer called to remind me that I had agreed to chaperone my son's ninth-grade dance, I sincerely said, "What are you, NUTS?!"

To which she replied, "That's what all the parents say, which is why we took fingerprints. It's you, all right, and your husband.

"There must be some mistake. I'm sure I signed up for paper sorter."

"We word it that way. How else would we get any volunteers?" she laughed.

The ride to the dance, with my son and his friend in the back seat, was relatively quiet, except for the sound of them trying to stay on the leather seat. With all that gel in their hair, they were sliding around like a couple of greased pigs.

Before we even parked the car, they rolled out the door and disappeared into the crowd waiting at the school entrance.

Within minutes, my husband and I were swept into the gymnasium, where a DJ was spinning CDs. It was obvious this was his part-time job and he was here to round up new customers for his daytime job at Miracle Ear.

Ninth graders swarmed into the gym and immediately found their personal huddles. It seems the wall is not the most popular place at dances these days. It's the huddle. Everybody stands in huddles on the floor. The huddles were so tight you couldn't see who was in the middle.

Some braver souls actually wandered outside the huddles and attempted to look in. But this was obviously a no-no, because a huddle of football players picked me up and huddled me to the other side of the gym where the chaperones were supposed to stand. This was teen territory and we parents were definitely the misfits, the outsiders. Our clothes fit too well. Our shoes were too low.

The girls greeted each other with screeches and screams of surprise, as if it were their tenth reunion, instead of only two hours since they said good-bye at the bus stop.

Of course, all the guys were showing off, big time, by standing there—shoulders slouched, hands in their pockets—and wearing the well-practiced facial expression of a worm.

The most stunning realization was the range of maturity among ninth graders. They ranged from tadpoles to frogs with full beards. Voices as high and sweet as Sandy Duncan's intermingled with baritones likened to Larry King throughout the gym. And this was just from the guys!

My son, who stood in a huddle with his best friend, looked like Dudley Moore standing next to Shaquille O'Neal. He was the same size as his buddy's left bicep.

As for the girls, well, let's just say some could easily audition for *Baywatch* and some for *Barney*.

I was attempting to pick out my son's future bride, when

POOF! The lights went out. All the girls screamed. It was madness and mayhem. Suddenly, we had a reason for being there.

"Come on, Tony, I waved to my husband. We've got to get this crowd under control." Without waiting for him, I swooped into the crowd and began patting shoulders and saying, "Okay, everybody calm down! Calm down! It's just a minor technicality. I'm sure they'll get these lights back on any minute."

Suddenly, I felt someone bump into my shoulder. The crowd was getting unruly. I turned around ready with my fiercest chaperone stare.

It was the principal. "Excuse me, Mrs. DiSandro, the lights are supposed to go off."

"They are?"

"Yes, the kids dance with the lights off."

"Do you think that's a good idea? Aren't we asking for trouble?"

"Well, the only trouble brewing right now is that the kids, with your son in command, are getting ready to hang you from the basketball net."

"Oh, well, okay. I'll just move back to my post by the bleachers."

"How about taking up a new post in the coatroom," he suggested.

"But there's nobody in there."

"Exactly."

It seemed like a millennium before the dance ended and we were heading back to the car. In their own words, my son and his friend expressed their utmost enthusiasm over the event: "It was okay."

"Did you dance with anybody?" I asked.

"Mom," my son said. "Nobody dances!"

I turned to my husband. "What great philosopher said, 'The more things change, the more they stay the same'?"

My husband replied with certainty, "That's from a beer commercial, isn't it?"

TEEN CLIFFS NOTES

I'm sure one classic novel is on every teenager's high-school reading list, and just like in my day, the kids are in a panic. The definition of a classic is a long book with big words—very difficult to read while watching the *Brady Bunch*, which is how I read *Wuthering Heights* by Emily Brontë.

But I never made it past the first sentence. Let's face it. Classics can be real snoozers. They weren't written with a teenage mind in mind. And yet, who gets stuck—I mean, who gets the wonderful opportunity to read them the most? Teenagers. So I'm offering my services to the future leaders of America by writing teen versions of the classics. Here's my first in the series: *Wuthering Heights for Teenagers*.

The story takes place in England a long time ago—like, before they had cable—and is loosely based on the television show *Party of Five*.

The Earnshaw family's life story is told in a flashback from the maid's point of view, which, is like, soooo confusing, but totally necessary, because confusing the reader is what makes any book a classic.

The Earnshaws live in Wuthering Heights, a creepy-looking house on the moors. (Picture the Munsters on Mockingbird Lane, and if you can't picture that, check it out on Nick at Night. You'll laugh your nose ring off.) Daddy Earnshaw has just returned from a long business trip and the two kids, Cathy and Hindley, are going totally nuts because he promised to bring home presents. The hit toy of the 1800s, comparable to Nintendo 64, was probably, although I'm just guessing, a rock.

But the dad surprises them all with a kid instead. Talk about lame! Didn't anybody ever tell this guy that before making any major purchases, or bringing home a kid, you're supposed to first ask your wife? Obviously, they didn't know this in the nineteenth century, which is why they invented the couch.

The dad named the orphan kid Heathcliff. Cathy and Hindley didn't like him because he was dirty and didn't shop at Old Navy. But in time, Cathy and Heathcliff became best friends. Cathy grows up to be really phat, like Cindy Crawford. Hindley goes off to college, comes back with a wife, and inherits Wuthering Heights. He still doesn't like Heathcliff. So now that his parents have bit the dust, he makes Heathcliff sleep in the barn like the other field hands. Bummer.

Cathy is hanging out on the moors one day when she discovers a boy on the next moor named Edgar and decides to marry him . . . because he's rich and pretty fly for a white boy.

Nellie, the maid, asks, "What about Heathcliff?" Cathy says that she loves Heathcliff, but he's just a scrub, which is, like, sooo nasty.

Heathcliff is listening outside the door! He's, like, really bummed so he runs away.

Cathy marries and moves to the next moor—called Thrushcross Range—with Edgar and his sister, Isabella. Everything is fine until Guess Who? shows up, three years later, looking like a total hotty? Heathcliff. (The book doesn't actually say, but I think he made his fortune in teeth whitener.)

Well, Cathy is way too happy to see him. So Edgar and Heathcliff fight. Cathy is so upset she runs to her bedroom and locks the door and stays in there for a week—without pizza, television, telephone, or a CD player. And since it was before computers, she couldn't instant-message her best friends. So she nearly dies, which is, like, totally understandable.

To get his revenge on everybody for his rotten life, Heathcliff wins Wuthering Heights from Hindley in a card game after Hindley becomes a drunk because his wife died in childbirth. Hindley ignores his kid, Hareton, and, of course, the kid can't go to school with a name like Hareton, so he hangs on the moor.

To make Cathy jealous, Heathcliff marries Edgar's sister, Isabella. They have a kid, Linton, but Heathcliff can't stand him and treats him like your basic punching bag.

Then Cathy dies.

Hindley dies.

Isabella dies.

(*Note:* This was way before Tylenol so people croaked from head colds, fevers, and paper cuts.)

Cathy died while giving birth to a girl, named Cathy. Edgar raises her himself, hoping she never discovers her weirdo relatives on the next moor. But she does. And Heathcliff forces her to marry his wimpy son, Linton. Then Linton dies. So she notices Hareton. And just like a girl, she thinks she can change him. So she buys him some cargo pants, teaches him how to be fly, and they live happily ever after.

Oh, and Heathcliff dies, too, but not before he is haunted by the first dead Cathy, just like in the movie *Sixth Sense*. Talk about déjà vu!

The End

CHAPTER 8

Defends Time Alone

The phrase "working mother" is redundant. —Jane Sellman

UP ON THE ROOF

Do you know how sometimes you hear a song on the radio, or your child's Barney sing-along tape, and for the rest of the day you can't get the irritating melody out of your head? I'm experiencing a similar problem, only it's not a song. It's an image that's stuck in my head—an image of a woman sitting on a roof.

Early one summer evening, while strolling through my neighborhood, I came upon a woman sitting on the roof of her house. She was talking on a cordless phone and looked so relaxed it seemed as if she belonged there. I continued on my walk, until it registered, a few blocks later, that in our subdivision dotted with big wheels and baby strollers, this was not a common site.

This wasn't Chicago, with its flattop roofs, where residents sit to get a perfect view of Wrigley Field. It wasn't New York City, where couples in flowing gowns and black tuxedos dine under the stars while the notes of a solo violinist float toward the sky. Our slanted rooftops were not designed for sitting.

The woman's gray shingled roof was similar to all the others that top the two-story, aluminum-sided homes in our neighborhood. It was sloped at an angle, like my cutting board when I push a pile of freshly chopped green beans into a bowl waiting below. Some of the beans tumble down and over each other before my knife can sweep the more stubborn ones along. It was probably the roughness of the shingles, and the fact that she rested her feet in the gutter, that helped to keep her from sliding down to the front yard below.

Long after my walk was over, the image of the woman kept playing in my head. I'd see her sitting so calm and comfortable, with her feet in the gutter, talking on the phone. And the question gnawing at me is always the same: *What was she doing up there?!*

Was it a roofing problem? I wondered. A gaping hole or a few loose shingles might cause a person to climb up and take a look. And I suppose if they took a phone along, they could describe to the roofer exactly what the problem entailed. But a quick scan of the roof showed no discernable signs of wear.

Installing a satellite dish, maybe? Yet, no tool belt hung from her hips and no service van stood in the driveway.

It was too early in the fall for cleaning gutters. Perhaps she was retrieving an overthrown Frisbee, a couple of baseballs, or some end-of-the summer toys that had found their way up there.

But, then, why the phone? Oh no! Could she be on the phone with the crisis center and contemplating ending it all?!

Well, actually, she was on the lower roof, the one accessible through a bedroom window. It would've made a lot more sense for her to pick the higher roof for such a dramatic event.

Maybe she was a misplaced New Yorker, more at home on a rooftop than a backyard deck?

In order to put the image to rest, I've come up with my own explanation.

I imagine she's a mom. A mom who has heard the word "MOMEEEE!" bounce off the walls of every room in the house one too many times. A mom who cannot hold a phone conversation without hearing, "Where's my socks?" "Where's my homework?" "Where's my briefcase?" A mom in search of a tiny space of her own, where she can be unreachable and untouchable for an entire two minutes.

So she says to her friend, "Would you hold on a second?" She flees to her bedroom, pulls up the window, and walks out onto the roof.

Silence.

A cool breeze.

She sits down, rests her feet on the Beanie Babies in the gutter, and tells her friend, "Okay, go ahead. I can hear you now."

I imagine her kids and husband running through the house, opening closets and bathroom doors, yelling, "Moooom! Where are you?" The irritation in their voices evident, because they need those baseball pants washed for the game tomorrow, that permission slip signed for a field trip, and they can't find the can opener.

She sits calm and collected, perched upon the roof of her chaotic kingdom, letting the rulers of the roost fend for themselves for a while. Oh, she'll come down, eventually—after a long talk with her friend and after she fills her lungs with the end of summer. Maybe she'll wait until the sky turns dark so that she can wish upon on a star.

Sometimes, I have a notion to go up to her front door and ask, "Can you tell me why you were sitting on your roof the other day?"

But then I stop myself. I don't want to know that she was simply adjusting her antenna while talking to her husband in the living room below. I like to think her daring move gives us all permission to go up on the roof sometimes.

INFLUENTIAL NEIGHBORS

My new neighbor across the backyard, a bubbly blonde with the body of an athlete, wants to be my friend. Now, usually, I prefer friends who are more like me—brunette, crabby, with the body of a woman whose only sport is walking to the mailbox once a day—but I wanted to be neighborly, so I went over for a visit.

I learned that Kelly runs her own small business, like me. But since she's out of her pajamas by eight o'clock every morning; I'm fairly certain she's not a writer.

Kelly had this glow about her, which was really irritating and contrasted with my glower. She seemed to have the ability to handle almost any situation with a calmness and clarity. When her four year old plodded into the house covered in mud, she said sweetly, "Did you have a good time, honey?" Frankly, I was worried she was on something, and I thought, as a responsible neighbor, I should get to the bottom of it as quickly as possible, so that I could be on it too.

Kelly told me her attitude had to do with her business, and if I was interested, I could take a class. She led me to the studio in her house. There were pillows, blankets, and little mats—similar to the one I used in kindergarten—all over the floor. There was a candle in the corner, casting a calming light around the room, and one of those rock fountains trickling on a table. I stared in fascination.

"Sign me up," I gushed, anticipating the much-needed rest I would soon be enjoying. Kelly said to wear comfortable clothes, so the next afternoon, I just stayed in my pajamas and waddled across the backyard to her patio door.

As soon as I stepped into her studio, I sensed something was amiss.

"Why isn't everybody sleeping?" I asked in confusion.

"We don't sleep in yoga class," Kelly laughed.

"Yoga!" I gasped. "I thought you were a nap specialist."

Well everyone had a good laugh on me.

I quickly backed out of the room, but a Buddhalike bouncer stopped me and gently guided me to a mat. He said something about "in each pose you will find repose."

"What kinda hose?" I asked. "We better not have to wear pantyhose!" I warned, flopping down and hunching over my knees.

The class looked on in pity.

"I can see we've got a lot of work to do," Kelly sighed, pulling at my shoulders. "Didn't your mother ever tell you to sit up straight?"

This neighborly thing was not working out at all.

Soon Kelly had my body in positions I couldn't pronounce,

much less perfect. She didn't just want me to put my hands behind my back, she wanted me to put my body behind my back!

At one point, I was twisted tighter than a Twizzler stick.

"Now I'm going to let go," Kelly said, "and see if you can hold that pose." My body unwound faster than a kid on a twisted park swing. I whipped around and around, shot across the room, knocked over the candle, and landed with my head in the rock fountain.

Kelly immediately picked me up and positioned me in a pose that helps with headaches.

Surprisingly, it worked. I felt a calmness wash over me. My breathing came in deep, even breaths. I was so relaxed that I could've stayed there with my legs up in the air for hours, if the lady next to me hadn't pushed me over and told me to stop snoring.

I'm actually looking forward to the next class. Kelly says I'll soon have that glow. Meeting neighbors can lead to new paths in life. But my husband is wary about me getting to know the lady across the street. He heard she's a racecar driver.

THE GIRL WHO COULD MAKE HER MOM STOP YELLING

In my defense, I'm not a morning person—never was, never will be. If you ask my kids, they'd probably say my A.M. demeanor falls somewhere between a growling grizzly and the *Little Mermaid*'s Ursula the Sea Witch. Let's face it. Even on my good days, the only thing I have in common with Mary Poppins is a flair for hats.

Before I reach caffeine consciousness, I'm like a speedboat in low gear, rumbling and mumbling as I steer around the kitchen preparing lunch sacks and overseeing breakfast choices.

"Put that ice cream back! Have a piece of fruit instead of another bowl of that sugar!" It doesn't take long to switch into high gear. "Get back here and put your bowl in the dishwasher!" "Did you brush your teeth?" "You still have fifteen minutes before the bus, so march right up there and make your bed, Buster!"

I imagine that after twelve years of this sunny greeting to the new day, my two older children don't even hear me. They just see this head with the mouth opening and closing like a wide-mouth bass.

But my toddler, Jenna, I'm afraid, sees a piranha gobbling up all the little fishies in the family sea. In the middle of my morning tirade, Jenna interrupts, "Excuse me, Mom. Excuse me!"

"What??" I snap.

"Do you still love me?"

My trap shuts. "Of course, I still love you," I say, swallowing gulps of guilt. I suppose she figures that the two older kids have just written themselves out of the family will and she had better quickly assess her own situation and, just to be on the safe side, pack a bag for Grandma's.

That day, after Jenna's older brother and sister left for school, Jenna and I set out for the library (at least I couldn't yell in there). Picking out books with a toddler is a hit-or-miss thing, as you chase her around the tall shelves, steer her clear of the computers, and encourage her to finish puzzles. I barely glanced at the covers as I grabbed a handful of books from the bins, until the drawing of the little boy staring up at his mother stopped me. The title of the book was *The Boy Who Could Make His Mother Stop Yelling*, by Ilse Sondheimer.

"The boy was Danny, and his mother was a very, very big lady," the first page read, showing a black-and-white sketch drawing of Danny and his "big" mother standing back to back.

The book went on to say that Danny's mother had two voices: "One was soft like a blue blanket . . . and the other was big like a lion's." It turns out that Danny's mom had given birth to his new baby brother and she was a little on edge. (Well, you don't need a new baby to be on edge, just a full schedule, three kids, and a husband out of town for three days—or sometimes just a mom who forgets the sizes of things.)

At one point in the story, Danny is afraid to tell his mother that he can't find his raincoat. He starts to cry, and to his surprise, he finds his "big" mother sitting at the kitchen table crying too.

That's when I started crying. And just like Danny, Jenna

climbed into my lap and hugged me tight. "What's wrong, Mom? Is the lady sick?" she asks.

"No, she just feels bad for yelling?"

"Oh."

"Does your mommy yell like that?" I ask.

"Yup."

"How does she do it?"

"Like this, 'Go do your homework!' Jenna shouted while wagging her finger.

"Does it scare you?" I ask.

"Yup."

Now, I'm left with a choice. I can give my daughter a big explanation about how sometimes a parent must yell to get her point across. I can tell her that her brother and sister made me do it because they don't listen. I can tell her that I don't really mean it, so it doesn't count. But I know these are answers that will only make me feel better. The answer she needs to hear is simple and direct.

"I'm sorry."

"That's okay, Mom," Jenna says, hugging me.

I look into her eyes and see that it really is okay.

"Let's read another book," I suggest.

We close the book on the last page, with Danny and his mother dancing around the kitchen.

Suddenly, I feel like dancing too.

WRITE BRAIN NEVER CLOSES

"I want you to write Oprah for me," my sister announced while I sat inhaling my mother's creamy, dreamy potato salad.

"Of course, the deadline is tomorrow, so you'll have to help me with it right now!" she explained, pulling the fork from my mouth and replacing it with a pen.

"But this (chew, chew, savor, savor) is my vacation and I'm busy (chew, chew, savor, savor) eating mother's creamy, dreamy potato salad!" I explained.

"It's not like you have to exert yourself," my sister said defensively. "Just tell me what to say and I'll write it down. It's that simple."

"But, but, it's my day off!"

"But if you tell Oprah how disorganized my house is, she'll send someone over to clean it up. Of course, I haven't heard anything about the last contest you helped me with. So this time, could you write it stronger, better, well, you know, like Hemingway or Danielle Steele?"

Once you admit to being a writer, or even a humor columnist, everyone assumes you can write—anything, anytime, anywhere and any way they want it. So they bring their scribbled resumes and sketchy grant applications to graduation celebrations, family birthdays, and Uncle Mario's foot surgery, and say, "Could you punch this up for me, Deb? And make me sound scholarly."

A hairstylist can say, "I'm sorry, I left my scissors at home." A doctor can say, "Why don't you stop by my office some morning next week and we'll have a look."

But what can I say? "Let me check and see if I brought my brain with me. Nope, it seems to be missing. I must've left it on my desk, under the big bust of Erma Bombeck."

My mother shoves a get-well card under my nose. "I want to add something caring but encouraging. You write it, but don't mess it up. The man is sick, you know!"

My husband shows me his speech for a conference: "I know it's incredible already, but if you want to punch it up, I wouldn't mind."

I've punched up, jazzed up, dreamed up, and cleaned up letters of recommendation, biographies, and birth announcements during baby showers, football games, and funerals, with the client hovering directly over my writing muse. (And I thought editors were hard to please.)

"No, that stinks! Give it some zing," my sister complains. "That cheesy sentence doesn't express how I feel. It needs to be more like Dave Barry. Are you sure you know what you're doing?"

"This is just the first draft," I explain.

"Well how many drafts do you need to write?"

"I'm not sure."

"I thought professional writers just zipped through these things."

"We don't zip," I explained. "We think."

"Well think faster. The deadline is tomorrow."

My twenty-year-old second cousin called the other day. "I didn't get the restaurant manager position. They said the resume you wrote lacked substance."

"Well, if I remember correctly, the only substance I had to work with was the one day you worked at Ponderosa."

"Couldn't you have embellished it a bit?"

"Calling you an 'experienced connoisseur of American cuisine' was the best I could do."

When I tell people at a party that I write, they immediately position the "guest with a book" at my table. Before I can protest and explain that I'm just a humor columnist, the "guest with a book" is pleading with me to take a look.

"Okay," I shrug. "Sure, I'll read your book. Where is it?"

"Oh, I didn't write it yet. It's all up here," the author says, pointing to the thinking space just above his eyebrows. "I'll give you a brief synopsis."

Six hours later, he's still synopsizing.

"Gosh, I hate to cut you short," I say while leaping for the door. "You've got a real page-turner there, but you might want to see if there's a renewed interest in how to make jewelry out of gallstones."

At night, before I lay my creative *write* brain down to sleep, my toddler says, "Read me a story, Mom."

"How about the *Three Little Pigs?*" I yawn.

"No!" she demands. "One of *your* stories."

She means a made-up story, one that will require my write brain to stay open for another hour.

"Once upon a time, there was a girl named Jenna who lived in a shoe. She had so many children she didn't know what to do."

I waited to see if Jenna would notice the familiar story line.

She didn't utter a word.

Well, I sighed to myself. *Not everyone's a critic.* I quickly wrapped up the familiar rhyme and said, "Goodnight," while kissing her forehead.

As I walked out of the room, Jenna called out, "Goodnight, copycat!"

SLIGHTLY OFF THE WALL

I was hanging out in the bathroom, the room in my house where most of my revelations take place, when I made a startling discovery: I had become an accomplished artist. Of course, nobody knew it, besides me. But if van Gogh, Monet, or Michelangelo could see the spectacular walls of my bathroom, they'd recognize the color and composition, technique, and texture of a fellow artist.

Yes, if my walls could talk, they'd surely say, "Leave us alone, lady!"

But alas, I cannot, because a white wall is my blank canvas and a voice deep inside me says, "You must paint! Or live with these dirty white walls."

So I dipped into my palette of Butter Yellow mixed with Lemon Glaze and applied it to my walls in brave, bold, sweeping strokes. As I employed this color-washing technique, indicative of the Impressionist period, I was at one with Monet. And when I began to stencil a pattern on the opposite wall, the masterpiece took shape. What Monet did for haystacks, I did for rubber duckies. I painted a series of those cute little duckies from different angles—here a ducky, there a ducky, everywhere a ducky, ducky. The fractured light glinting off the soap scum spoke volumes.

As I stretched my body and brushed toward the ceiling, I was in tune with Michelangelo and knew exactly what he was thinking while painting the Sistine Chapel: "Gee, if only I were a little taller."

My walls are alive with color—Vivacious Violet, Samba Sage, and Peachy Passion. There are no safe colors in my house. My husband says, "No wall is safe in our house." Yes, just like the dispirited van Gogh, my talent is often misunderstood. My husband never truly appreciated the pink and blue-green fish sponged onto the guest-room walls, even when I explained that it had been directly inspired by Suerat's Pointillism method.

He claims the marbleized Wild Berry walls in our dining room cast a sick color on his food and he can't eat. And my preschooler took one look at her newly painted bedroom, with the swirling bubblegum-colored walls accented by squiggly lime-green stripes (my own version of van Gogh's, the *Starry Night*), and said, "Gee, Mom, I could've done that myself."

Obviously, this world was never meant for walls as beautiful as mine.

I'll admit, not every one of my walls is destined for greatness. But it helps to remember that art is about passion not perfection. All I have to do is paint the slate clean and begin again. No one is the wiser, especially if I hide the receipt from Menards.

AND THE PERISHABLES GO TO . . .

Although the moving van blocked the usual view from my office window, I caught a glimpse of my neighbor's daughter as she struggled across the street, carrying a large white garbage bag. She plopped her heavy load on my front step and rang the bell. I smiled as I greeted her, reaching out to grab the awkward gift as she shoved it through the door.

"Thank you, Carly," I said while dragging the cool bag across the floor and into the kitchen.

There was no need to say more. I knew the contents and their proper destination.

"Why don't you go and find the kids," I suggested. "I'll call and tell your mom you'll be staying for lunch."

She skipped off while I bent down to open my present. Half bottles of ketchup, mayonnaise, and enough pickle relish for a hot dog or two. I was surprised by the German mustard; I would've taken Jeannette for a honey-mustard person. Hmmm . . . a new brand of toaster pastry with eggs and green pepper. *I'll have to try that for breakfast,* I thought as I continued digging into the bag and then pushing and cramming my newly acquired treasures into the open spaces in my fridge.

I was the recipient of my neighbor's refrigerator. The last vestiges, the stuff worth saving but not toting to another state, the perishables went to me.

It's an intimate thing, this glimpse into the recesses of someone's fridge. You don't give the contents to just anyone. The honor goes to the one who wouldn't judge you if the cap on the ketchup bottle was crusty or smirk when she discovered you used imitation crabmeat in that wonderful casserole.

The perishables are awarded to the neighbor you weren't

embarrassed to bother when you locked yourself out of your house for the second time in one week. The one who took in your mail when you went out of town and kept watch on your empty house and your favorite rosebush. I should know; I gratefully presented the award myself a time or two.

But this time, I was learning how to be on the receiving end. I learned that when your new neighbor comes welcoming you to the neighborhood, you must call soon after, believing her when she says, "If there's anything you need . . ."

You won't mind sending your kid over to borrow her last onion for your beef casserole, because you'd gladly give her your last egg for her son's birthday cake. In a short time, you've worn a path to her door. You trust her with an extra key to your house. You use her name as your emergency contact on school papers. You feel comfortable enough to cry at her kitchen table on an, "I'm such a rotten mother" day. Your families share more than a few meals together and sometimes you laugh together until your sides ache. You cry the day her "for sale" sign goes up and raise a cheer when she calls to tell you she has a buyer. You hold back the tears until you hang up.

Now, I knew about both sides of the move. As I sat sorting through the perishables, memories of my own move, a few months before, began to surface. At that moment, I knew how it felt to be completely in someone else's skin. I could envision my neighbor across the street, cleaning out her fridge, cleaning behind the movers as they emptied all the familiar spaces, memories flooding as she wiped the wet cloth across the baseboards, pushing back the tears while trying to grasp how to get from moving to moving on.

My fridge was finally full. I stood up with a sigh and closed the door. Soon, now. Soon, I would walk the familiar path for the last time. I knew my role too well. I was to take the last peek. She would need to hear my voice echo off the bare walls, "Everything looks beautiful! The new owners will love it."

Then I would go home, and a couple of days after a new moving van pulls up, I'll open the fridge and pull out the butter for the cookies that I'll bake and carry across the street to welcome our new neighbors with those familiar words: "If there's anything you need . . ."

GARAGE SALES AND GUILT DON'T MIX

After unloading the back of my minivan for the fifth time one week, I've decided garage sales are not for the guilt ridden. As a mother of three, my life is awash with guilt. And although I try to leave it at home, when I garage sale, waves of it follow me. When I saunter up someone's driveway, an ocean of guilt dumps itself right in my purse.

As I stand there fingering someone's chipped knickknacks, rickety roller skates, and toys loved to a tattered state, it suddenly dawns on me that I have the exact same stuff piled up in my own garage. Only instead of being in the comfort and safety of my own garage, I'm stuck smack dab in the middle of a garage that belongs to some stranger who's desperately hoping to sell enough stuff to send her whole family to Disney World!

The guilt pours out of my purse as I attempt to inch my way out of the garage and down the driveway. I can feel the eyes of the owner searing into my departing, quivering frame, pulling me back with a force stronger than that of a ride on Space Mountain. So I grab the nearest item and bring it up to the cigar-box register.

"She's stealing my Boo-Boo Bunny, Mommy! Stop her! Stop her!" The proprietor's daughter cries as I race down the driveway.

Suddenly, I'm Cruella DeVil incarnate.

The owner (a mom with her own ocean of guilt) chases me down, grabs Boo-Boo, slaps fifty cents into my empty hand, and sobs, "I'm so sorry. It's her Boo-Boo. I didn't think she played with it anymore."

"But I gave you a dollar!" I shout.

Now the mother, child, and Boo-Boo are all hugging and kissing. I'd feel guilty if I intruded, but I only got paid for one Boo.

At my next stop, I find myself stuck in a garage filled with hand-me-downs, handed down one-too-many times.

"Things are pretty picked over," the woman says. "My sister

took most of the stuff for her daughter, but my Jessie here want-ed to sell her old clothes so she could buy an American Girl doll." A cute, little four year old smiles up at me with the biggest brown eyes I've ever seen. (Aw, gee, why did she have to wear those winter boots in the middle of summer? They made her look so adorably pathetic.)

Her mom says, "She's been so determined since her operation."

Well, that did it. A tidal wave gushes out of my purse. "Just pack it all up and put it in the van," I say. "How much do you want? Fifty? One hundred? Would you take those boots off your little girl, please, before I go broke?"

When an entire block holds a garage sale, I always feel sorry for the one without any customers.

"Let's go to this garage, kids."

"But she only has a few junky things, Mom."

"Marcus," I chastise my son, "someone else's junk may be our treasure. Besides, she looks so sad sitting there with no one walk-ing up to her garage. She needs us." So I walk up and grab the first thing I lay eyes on.

"What do you want with my rake?" the elderly woman asks.

"I'd like to buy it, of course." I practically have to wrestle her to the ground to get it out of her hands. "How much do you want for it?"

"Nothing," she shouts, staring at me as if I'm Freddy Krueger's cousin, "I'm not even in the garage sale!"

Sometimes I feel so guilty that I even convince the sellers not to sell.

"Madge, come quick. Do you see what she's buying?" the lady at the cigar-box register calls to her friend.

Madge's eyes well up with tears. "It's little Sandy's first birth-day dress. She was the cutest baby in the world. I hope your baby will do it justice."

Guilt button fully activated, I say, "Are you sure you really want to sell it?" She breaks into tears, blubbering all over the asphalt. "Why don't you wrap it in tissue and save it for your first granddaughter," I suggest, pulling a Kleenex from my purse and dabbing her eyes. "There, there, it'll be alright," I encourage. "Look, I'll just take this, uh, uh, little blow-up swimming pool here."

I felt so terrible; I didn't even ask if it leaked.

It leaked.

BRING BACK GRANDMA'S BEAUTY SHOP

There was one thing I could count on as a child, no matter what catastrophe transpired during the week—whether the country went to war or aliens invaded the earth, landed in our backyard, and held us captive in their spaceship—come Saturday morning, Mom and Grandma would show up at the beauty shop—nine o'clock sharp. Suddenly possessed with powers and abilities far beyond those of any mortal women, they'd run faster than a speeding bullet, leap tall buildings in a single bound, and waste aliens with a mean swing of their purses in order to uphold their hair-raising ritual.

Grandma's weekly special was the standard Fifty-and-Over Pin-Curl Set: little silver clips wound into her hair so tightly, I believe, it numbed her brain for at least twenty minutes (which was the window of opportunity I had to ask for a quarter for the pop machine). Then she'd plaster a piece of fishnet over it and say, "Don't want to get it mussed."

Mussed? Grandma's hair wouldn't have budged if a tornado touched down next to her purse.

My mother, like all hip moms of the '70s, wanted a beehive. The higher the better. The beauty operator would tease and rat a ball of fur, which she would then attached to Mom's own hair with clasps closely resembling the machine screws from my father's toolbox.

I felt it my responsibility to yell, "Duck!" whenever she approached doorways and viaducts with clearances of under ten feet.

As we left the beauty shop, Mom and Grandma each pulled tiny pieces of plastic from the deep recesses of their purses. With a quick shake, the tiny plastic squares magically billowed out into rain hats with the same dimensions as your basic blimp. They quickly tied them under their chins like bonnets. Fearing a sudden liftoff, I always prayed for a windless day.

Today, beauty shops are called salons. And hair is never "set" but "styled." We all ask for the standard fast-food fare: an Every-Six-Week Cut-and-Blow-Dry Combo. We're out quicker than the two-piece suit at the dry cleaners across the street.

So why do I yearn for a beauty-shop appointment? Because after a long afternoon away from home, Mom and Grandma always came back smiling and giggling. They felt as pretty and pampered as two schoolgirls on prom night.

It was the ultimate mini-spa. A place where women of all ages and stages of beauty convened for a short retreat from the pressures of work and motherhood. Back when beauty shops were beauty shops, no one talked about St. John's Wart. The gentle yet firm motion of nimble fingers washing your hair and massaging your scalp eased tensions. Problems trickled down the sink with the soapsuds. And since it took time to wrap silky strands of wet hair around different sized rollers and clips, beauty operators became a captured audience and often lent a sympathetic ear. Then, under the hooded warmth and hum of hair dryers, women reveled in thirty minutes of much-needed solitude. Afterward, they felt refreshed, and hopefully—if they had a decent operator—they looked good too!

Now I understand why Mom and Grandma held so fiercely to their Saturday ritual. It was more than a new hairdo; it was a weekly reminder for women to take care of themselves. Seems a simple but smart solution to the stresses of today—the ritual, not the beehive.

CHANGING OF THE PURSE

"It's really hot in here!" I said, looking for a place to sit down.

"I feel shaky myself," my mother agreed. "But we've got to get through this."

"Why? Why does it have to be this way?" I complained while fanning my flushed face with a store sales ad.

Speaking from years of experience, my wise mother explained,

"There is no other way, honey." She patted my arm and assured me, "Together, we'll beat this thing."

My mother and I were going through "the change." And as any woman knows, it can be a long and difficult process. Let's face it. No woman willingly begins "the change." It's obviously propelled by a force of nature greater than we are.

When my mother and I saw the ad, we realized we had no choice but to yield to the mighty power of fifty to seventy percent off. So, reluctantly, but with some hope for the future, we began "the change": the changing of the purse.

Your purse fits you like a second skin. Losing it is incomprehensible. But shedding it, even when you know you'll be replacing it, can cause anxiety, tremors, and even hot flashes.

We walked into the purse department with trepidation and some anticipation. There was always the hope, however slim, that we might find an even better skin graft than before.

To begin our search, we went our separate ways. We would seek each other out when we needed support. The standards a purse must meet are very personal. It's not just a matter of size or color. There's the strap, squish, dangle, weight, zipper, and snap-and-compartment tests, to name just a few.

After a few hours on my own, I found one worthy of a second opinion. "What do you think of this one?" I asked my mother.

"It looks good on you," she smiled.

This one passed the preliminaries. It was ready for the mirror test. I examined it from every angle. I walked. I sauntered. I jogged in place. I dug inside. I opened and closed, opened and closed.

"Darn it!" I cried, tossing it back on the display rack. "It's too narrow."

"For your wallet?" my mother asked.

"No, to partially cover my left thigh."

She nodded in complete understanding. "I almost chose this one," she said, holding up a tan and navy bag, "but it failed the airport-strap test."

I nodded sympathetically. "It's too short to hang around your neck and across your chest when walking through a crowded environment, like the airport."

"Exactly," Mom agreed.

The biggest test for both of us was the compartment compatibility check. My mother needed a compartment for her cell phone and a large midsection for photos of her grandchildren from every angle and age, plus a snap purse on the front to carry her loose change. I needed a zipper insert along the inside for my business cards, a midsection long enough to fit my wallet, and an ample sidecar for all of my husband's and kids' stuff.

It took two long days for the transformation to take place, but my mother and I finally found our second skins.

Or so we thought.

After living with her purse for a shopping trip or two, my mother realized she had neglected to perform the squishing test, and her new skin didn't squish to her specifications. Alas, she returned it. The salesperson, a squisher herself, totally understood.

Although still adjusting to my new gray, leather skin, I believe the graft is taking. I can stuff three happy-meal toys, my husband's allergy inhaler, and my daughter's math homework in and still close it.

A few days later, my mother called to tell me she had bought a new purse. I was deeply hurt that she had made the change without me, but I understood. We all must go through the change in our own way and in our own time.

COOKING WITH A BURNING PASSION

Whenever I want a good laugh, I turn on the food channel and talk back to the chefs on television.

"Hey, Mr. Chef, in your starched, white apron! If you want to truly test your culinary skills, try slapping together that soufflé while a toddler bangs all your shiny pots and pans on the floor, a beginning pianist tortures eighty-eight keys, and a third grader shouts out a math story problem! Let's see how many teaspoons of fresh-ground pepper you put in then, huh, huh, huh? Come closer to the screen, so I can slap you with a sprig of cilantro!"

Anyone can be a chef, if they cook without kids.

I cook with a burning passion and frequently cry while dicing. The burn is heartburn from the background noise of a mutilated

Beethoven sonata with a pot-and-pan bass-drum accompaniment and a kid shouting, "If a train is going sixty miles per hour for 666 hours and another train is going two miles per hour on an ice-frozen track, how many people are inside the train?" Believe me when I say the crying has absolutely nothing to do with onions. I cry because, after sixteen years of cooking for my family, I can honestly say, "I hate to cook."

I hate the whole planning, preparing, dicing, slicing, chopping, baking, boiling mess of it.

I once read that the Golden Gate Bridge is painted every single day, because as soon as the painters get to the other end, the bridge needs to be painted all over again. That's the first accurate description of cooking I've ever come across. Now, whenever I cook, I imagine myself dangling from the Golden Gate Bridge with a stalk of celery in my hand.

My day can be going along quite nicely and then I remember I haven't defrosted anything for dinner. So I open the freezer and stare inside. My eyes glaze over like the orange sauce on a Cornish hen. (I've never actually cooked one, but I've seen it on television.)

I drag myself to the pantry, pull out one of my fifty cookbooks, and flip through the pages. But they all seem to include one ingredient I never have on hand—a willing chef.

The magazines at the grocery checkout counter proclaim you can make dinner in minutes. So I eagerly toss them in my cart along with the Hamburger Helper. Then I get home, read the recipes, and wonder how I'm going to make Brazilian Black-Bean Bake in ten minutes if I have to go to Brazil to get the beans!

The recipes always call for these completely obscure ingredients, like saffron threads, fennel fronds, and salt. They never use the staples I already have in my kitchen, like cheddar-flavored goldfish and ding-dongs.

And, hey, if Rice-a-Ripoff or any of those other guys are going to put a recipe on the back of the box, then everything should be in the box, including the chopped Kalamata olives!

Personally, my favorite recipe has two—count 'em, two—ingredients: a phone and a phonebook. I don't envy celebrities like Oprah, their fame, or fortune, just their live-in cooks. But until I have my own talk show, it's back to fixing tonight's dinner: Ding-dong cheddar-cheese potato-chip soufflé surprise. If it turns out the way I'm hoping, my family will be ordering from the China Wok down the street.

PHOTO STITCHES IN THE FABRIC OF OUR LIVES

"Wait! Don't take any pictures today," I pleaded with my husband.

"But it's our son's first piano recital," he reminded me.

"I know, honey. But I'd like to get our photo album caught up before we capture anymore darn memories."

"Well, how many photos behind are you?" he asked.

"About thirteen years' worth."

Once again, I found myself on the cutting edge of a new trend. Reminiscent of the long-ago days when women gathered round a community table to stitch fabric squares into treasured quilts, this latest trend had me cropping, chopping, and mounting memories into creative, eye-catching photo albums.

The class at the local college promised to help me get my pictures out of boxes and into albums. The albums that the expert displayed were masterpieces on paper—acetate-free, of course. Die-cut hearts, stars, or oval shapes framed the photos and splashes of colored construction paper—pH balanced, of course—were used for background. Decorative stickers added the irresistible finishing touch.

My first thought was: "I want to do that!" My second thought quickly followed: "I can't do that!" But like the memory preservers who lived before me, I felt it my duty to be the preserver of family history, the glue stick that held together generations of the Dempsey and DiSandro clans.

My project began with organizing thirteen years of photos. I sorted chronologically by holidays, family vacations, and birthdays. Then, with my photo page, pen, and mounting corners in hand, I started to create my own memory album. After a few pages of artfully arranged photos, I realized that, had I sat at the quilting table with my pioneer pals from long ago, I would have been the one, who consistently and enthusiastically sewed my patchwork square securely to my petticoat.

"What are you chopping up all of our photos for?" my husband asked while peering over my shoulder.

"It's called cropping; I'm cutting all the insignificant stuff out of the pictures to focus on the most important parts."

"I don't think my uncle would consider his head unimportant."

"Well, I didn't want his bald spot to be the focal point."

"Our daughter looks cross-eyed in this picture," he added.

"It's the first time she saw her hand."

"But she looks terrible."

"That's not the point, honey. We're capturing special memories."

"Well, couldn't we capture the ones where we all look good?" he said, walking away.

Okay, maybe my albums wouldn't win any prizes, but the photos were going where they belonged, inside a book instead of under my bed in a box. To keep me motivated, I invited a friend over who was also interested in scrapbook keeping.

"Wow," I said as I watched her wheel in her box on a dolly. "After only four years of marriage and two children, you sure have a lot of photos."

"Oh, these aren't all of my pictures," she laughed. "These fifteen volumes just chronicle the birth of our first child."

We worked at the kitchen table long into the night, piecing together the fabric of our lives. We shared our favorite pictures and the stories that went along with them.

"This is my favorite photo of my daughter," I said holding it up for her to see.

"Awww, was it the first time she found her hand?"

"That's right!" I said, delighted that she understood.

"I have that same shot of my son, too—from sixty-seven different angles."

At our second scrapbook session, we talked of fire drills and escape routes to protect our growing memories from harm.

"I keep the albums right below the window in my office. Then if I have to jump out the upstairs window, I can run across the grass to my office, break the window, and scoop up my albums."

"I held a fire drill the other day," I confessed. "Every family member's been designated a specific album."

As we laughed at our photos, I imagined the women who came before us having the same conversation as they stitched the fabric of their generations into colorful quilts. It wasn't the material they treasured; it was the memory of Grandma's gingham apron, or the sight of their daughter in her first school dress, that held them steadfast to their work.

BE SELFISH—YOU OWE IT TO YOUR FAMILY

So you want to be a great mom? Then get away from your family. Yes, you heard me. Set a date and time to remove yourself from hubby and the kids. No, I don't mean forever, just long enough to take a few deep deep breaths, chew a couple of meals slowly, embrace the quiet of an afternoon, and get to know yourself again. Okay, that might take forever. But a weekend will help.

I spent last weekend at an old country inn, alone and by myself. The purpose, or so I thought, was to write. "A day and a half to write without distractions," I told my husband. "That's what I need."

Friday night, while preparing to leave, my husband, Tony, said, "I thought maybe me and the kids could drive you there and pick you up—to see what it's like and all." In the back of his mind, he was probably thinking, *If she doesn't have her own car, she can't drive off, take the first plane to Barbados, and leave me with the kids for an extra six days, or forever.*

In the back of my mind, I was thinking, *Darn! Now I can't drive off, take the first plane to Barbados, and leave Tony with the kids for an extra six days, or forever!* But I said, "Sounds great!"

After a thorough inspection of the room and grounds, my family seemed satisfied I'd survive without them. But I wasn't too sure. As I waved good-bye, guilt and fear overwhelmed me. "What was I doing? How could I leave them when, as it was, we had so little family time? What kind of mother was I?

A selfish one. An extremely selfish and totally terrified one at that! For the past ten years, I'd hardly the opportunity to go to the bathroom by myself and here I was spending the weekend alone.

Of course, slipping into the Jacuzzi eased my anxieties a bit. Yes, I said Jacuzzi. It wasn't my fault the only available tub featured warm jet streams that massaged every tired, aching joint and muscle. No impatient knocking on the door. No fighting outside the door. Although I knew it wasn't possible, I swore I heard a tiny voice shout, "MOM! I NEED YOU! NOW!"

Back in my room, decorated with flowers, lace, and dark antique furniture, I slipped back the crisp, fresh sheets on some great-grandma's wrought-iron bed and slept.

The next morning, I breakfasted at a long elegant table set with fancy-flowered china and red-colored goblets, and feasted on fresh strawberries and sweet watermelon, which to my delight somebody had cut into little slices for me! "Thank you! Oh, thank you!" I said to the lady of the house.

"You're welcome," she said, "but could you stop hugging me now?"

After breakfast, I took a stroll through the neighborhood. It felt odd to be walking without baby Jenna grasping my finger to steady herself, or my two older children Rollerblading beside me, but I breathed deeply, listened to the wind rustling through the towering trees lining the street, and found a pace of my own.

After my walk, I wrote for the entire afternoon. I can't say it was easy, but the fact that the television had awful reception and everybody in the inn knew I was supposed to be writing helped me to focus. What surprised me was the clarity of my thought processes. For once, I didn't have to stop to change a load of laundry or a diaper, to fix dinner or to break up the sixteenth sibling squabble of the day.

A nearby diner sufficed for lunch. I sat in a booth and read a book. Yes, I said read a book. And although I was tempted to tell the man at the next table to chew with his mouth closed, and to douse my napkin in the water glass and blot the ketchup off the server's apron, I resisted and focused on my own plate.

I wrote through the dinner hour and into the evening and then decided to take in a movie. Yes, I said, a movie, all by myself. Sure, it was uncomfortable saying, "One ticket, please," but it quickly faded when I realized the popcorn was all for me.

The next morning, I wrote again until my family bounded through the quiet inn to bring me back to my real world.

"MOM, Marcus tripped me!"

"It was an accident."

"No, it wasn't, you blockhead."

"You're the blockhead."

I hugged my blockheads to my chest and said, "Let's go home, blockheads. I missed you."

IS IT MY TURN?

The first love of my life is sick. The first man I thought truly handsome, with his thick shock of black, wavy hair and baby blue eyes, is in the hospital, in critical condition.

I sit by his bedside, helpless and afraid, wondering if there's something I should be doing to make this better. I stare into his blue eyes, filled with pain, and my heart hurts. It is going to break, I'm sure.

"What do you think of the surgeon?" he asks.

He's asking me? Oh, this is not right. I'm supposed to be the one asking questions. He answers them.

"He knows his stuff," I say with a conviction I don't feel.

When I can't be at his side, I must leave him in the hands of strangers. They care for him, but they don't know him. They don't know about his sense of humor and that a little girl learned the basics of being funny from this natural teacher. They haven't heard him use any of his unusual trademark sayings, such as, "I've known you since you were a pup!" or "I resemble that remark!" They don't know of his generosity and his love for his children and grandchildren. They don't know that he single-handedly organized a family reunion and then only attended it via phone from his hospital room.

I want to tell every nurse who too brusquely lifts his frail wrists to take his pulse, every aide who sighs when she must fix his pillows so that he doesn't develop bed sores, every nutritionist who can't seem to remember that he hates vanilla pudding and pudding is the only damn thing he can eat—I want to stop them all and say, "Excuse me, pardon me, please, but this man laying in this bed, this man is my father. My father. My daddy.

Once at home, I call every relative who's in medicine and ask tough hard questions about infections and such.

Please, someone tell me if this is going to be okay.

And I keep asking, "Is it my turn? Is it my turn?"

I've watched two of my close friends sit by their fathers' bedsides and finally losing them to cancer. I remember my mother's inconsolable crying when she lost her mother. I was twelve at the time, the same age my son is now.

Is it my turn? I ask.

I go through the motions of eating and preparing dinner, helping with homework, and visiting my daughter's school on parent night. When I walk into a restaurant and I see a healthy grandpa, with straight smooth hands and strong legs, I say, "Why? Why can't my children's grandpa have those hands, those legs, this moment, in this restaurant?"

Instead, my children make get-well cards, some computer-printed banners, and colorful posters to cover the four walls that surround their grandpa. I hang them above his hospital bed, so everyone knows this man is loved.

One night, during a terrible thunderstorm, my daughter, Lauren, stumbles into our bed. "I'm afraid," she says.

"I know," I say. And then I remind her of how much Grandpa loves a good thunderstorm. I hear the hail against the window and remember standing on the front porch with my father, thousands of storms ago, catching the pieces in my hand, while my mother cowered inside the house next to a lit candle. He saw the beauty in a storm, and to this day, they don't really frighten me.

No, that's not entirely true. Some storms can still scare me.

Is it my turn?

I count the hours until I can be with him again. The next time, I bring an electric razor that he asked for. We put it on his nightstand, next to his bottle of Old Spice. I sniff the air, to see if I can smell the familiar scent my dad wore the day I was born and the day he walked me down the aisle, but the smells of the hospital are more powerful.

We watch the baseball game together while he dozes in and out of a restless sleep. I lift his cup to his dry, cracked lips. I exchange his vanilla pudding for chocolate. I encourage him to finish his energy drink, although every sip causes him to swallow in agony. I need to leave for a while, so I walk down the hall for a coffee I can't taste.

I come back, stand outside his door, and slip on the gloves and gown necessary to walk into his room.

I sit again.

It's not like the movies. There isn't that one glowing moment when the picture softens and your dad whispers some words of wisdom and comfort, or the daughter finally understands what is happening, or some problem you've had gets resolved and he reaches out and holds your hand. It's not beautiful and it's not comforting.

The only thing I can say as I gulp back the giant rock in my throat is: "I love you, dad." And he whispers the same.

Is it my turn?

And the voice answers back, "Yes, yes, I believe it is."

MOVING ON

On a warm sunny day in September, I lost my father. I always thought it odd to use the word "lost" when referring to death. But it's the right word. My father is lost—to me, most definitely.

At the home he shared with his wife, I walk into the office where he created his computer-printed cards and labels, and he is not there.

Excuse me, but where did my father go? I know he was here just a minute ago. Here, look. He was getting ready to make these address labels with the cute little cartoon dog. See?

And look at this. Here's his handwriting on a note to me: *"Dear Deborah, how about a column about telephone charges? See my latest bill. Can anybody really understand the charges?"*

And over there, in the corner, are my columns, all neatly copied, organized, and stored in black binders by my father's hands.

It's been almost four weeks now. The constant reliving of the last few days of his life has finally loosened its grip on my dreams and my every waking thought. But it will never completely leave me, that moment when I stood by his bed and watched life drain from his beautiful face.

His wife tells me she talks to him out loud and it gives her comfort.

A friend tells me a shadowy figure appeared to her a few weeks after her own father's death.

Another friend sends me a book about life after death and another suggests a book on the process of grieving.

In the many sympathy cards that fill my mailbox, I'm told memories are the thing to hold onto.

But for me, there are no dark figures, no talking out loud, no books, no memories that can change what I most want to change. I want one more moment. One more hug. One more kiss. One more time for the phone to ring on a Sunday morning and hear his soft-spoken voice say, "Hello, it's your father. This is your Sunday-morning call."

No, that wouldn't be enough. At thirty-nine, I want my daddy back. All of him. That's it.

When I was a little girl, I would tell people that my father's name was Jack Dempsey, they would often reply, "Do you mean Jack Dempsey the boxer?" I always loved that, people thinking my dad was a famous prizefighter.

Of course, after a pause, I'd have to reply, "No, he's not *that* Jack Dempsey."

But he was a prize. And he was a fighter. He battled the ravages of rheumatoid arthritis for twenty-five years and never complained. "I'm alright. I'm fine," he'd insist, dismissing our looks of concern with a sweep of his crippled hand.

He fought alcoholism and won. He was one of the few people I knew who not only admitted his mistakes, but also sought to make amends for them throughout his life.

He was a quiet man and knew a thing or two about chivalry. He treated people with respect, and women, well, he just had a way of making you feel like the sweetest and most special lady on the face of the earth.

He found joy in the simple things: watching *Jeopardy* with his wife, Charlotte, being the first visitor to see a new grandchild, digging into a big dish of ice cream. And lunch with his daughters and grandchildren was a day to hold dear. As we kissed good-bye after an uneventful afternoon of food and talking, he'd say, "This . . . (the words stuck in his throat and his blue eyes filled with tears) this was a great day."

My father once told me that everyone should have three wishes. "You could write a column about it, Deborah. I think it's important."

"What are your three wishes, Dad?" I asked.

He smiled. "To take a cruise to Alaska, ride in a hot-air balloon, and . . ." he chuckled, "I want to chop down a tree with a chainsaw—not a live one of course," he added.

In August, after he was released from a forty-two-day hospital stay, I tried to think of a way to fulfill one of his wishes. He wasn't well enough to travel, but I thought an electric knife and a cake shaped like a tree log might at least simulate his third wish. And my father would truly appreciate the ingenuity and humor behind it. But before I could put my plan into action, he was back in the hospital for the final time.

When my father looked up at his family surrounding his bedside for his last moment on Earth, he tried to say something but couldn't talk. Yet, I think we all knew what he would've said. My father, an unselfish man, was trying to say, "Okay, everybody. My wonderful ride is up. Now go home and get on with your own lives."

So I'm going, Dad. I'm going home to find my three wishes, to look for joy in the simple things, and to be with my family. And if—when I leave this earth—my children adore me half as much as I did you, then I'll have had a wonderful ride too.

CHAPTER 9

Survives the Holi-daze

Love's a thing that's never out of season.   —Barry Cornwall

A MOM WITH A WINNING STROKE

Hardly a kid growing up today will get past the age of six or seven without some formal swim lessons. And most of these kids' moms, watching from the sidelines, are dog paddlers at best.

These moms all share the same conviction, "I want my kids to learn how to swim. I don't want them to be afraid like I was." But there comes a point in every person's life when she makes a choice whether to stand on the sidelines and watch or to jump in.

My friend Carol decided to jump in feet first into ten feet of water, with a floatie and a swimming instructor treading nearby.

Doesn't sound like much of a risk? Well, to understand the courage it took, you have to know the about the years of humiliation Carol suffered at the hands of her so-called "swimming friends." You have to know about the poolside humor at her expense—and about the fear.

Growing up, the most dreaded sweltering summer afternoons for Carol were the days her friend's cried, "Let's go to the pool!"

"Come on, guys," she'd say. "Let's do something else. How about baseball or climbing trees?"

My friend wasn't a timid girl who spent her days dressing Barbies. I had personally witnessed her conquering many daring feats, things usually referred to as "boys' stuff," like jumping off garage roofs and lighting firecrackers. But water had conquered her.

We, her friends, tried to teach Carol to swim—honest we did—when we weren't laughing so hard. Her flailing attempts at dog paddling would put most people in traction. She thrashed around like a kid caught in quicksand, and that was only in the baby pool.

Years later, everyone had a "Carol" water story. There was the time on vacation when, attempting to swim in a hotel pool, Carol suddenly shouted, "I'm drowning! I'm drowning! Help! Help!"

The lifeguard stood by, looking perplexed. He shook his head and shouted in Carol's direction. "Just stand up!"

So Carol did. And the water came to her waist.

Carol's family has their favorite story too. One morning her niece woke up to what sounded like a whole neighborhood of kids splashing around in the backyard pool. She came outside to find her Aunt Carol all by herself, attempting to sit on a floating raft.

"Help! I'm drowning!" Carol shouted, swallowing gulps of water.

Her niece calmly instructed her, "Just stand up."

Then, one day, Carol found herself in four feet of water with her baby in a swimming class:

"The instructor showed us how to hold the baby on her back," Carol recalled. "She told us to hold our babies with one hand. She said they would float. And I'm thinking, *are you sure? Are you sure she'll float?* I remember saying to myself, *I cannot be afraid to put my child in this amount of water. I've got to do something.*"

So Carol announced that she was taking swimming lessons. We had heard about her lessons over the years. But they never seemed to do much good and they never lasted for more than a few weeks.

So her husband laughed. Her family guffawed. And her friend, Deb, said, "Call me when you win the Olympic gold."

But then last summer, on a camping trip, Carol and her two children cried, "Let's go swimming!"

My friends and I watched her walk with her four year old and two year old down to the lake. We kept a close eye on her kids. We figured we might have to jump in at a moment's notice. But in a few minutes, our jaws dropped.

"Do you see what I see?" I nudged my friend Diana.

"Carol is swimming!" she gasped.

"Are you sure it's not a camping mirage?" I asked.

"Her stroke is better than mine, and look, she's going out to that raft!"

Later, I asked Carol what had happened to help her overcome her fear.

"Kids happened," she said, and then flashed back to that critical moment in the tenth week of her lessons:

"By that time I had mastered some swimming strokes and I could tread water, but it was the first time we were supposed to jump in the deep end of the pool. I was terrified. I stood there on the edge, asking the instructor all these questions, like I was a nut case, you know?"

"I know."

"He told me I might touch bottom and I was thinking, *Touch bottom! I don't want to touch bottom.* He assured me I would float back to the surface of the water, but I wasn't sure. I was shaking. Then I looked up and who was coming out of the locker room but my husband and two children.

"My husband says, 'Look, Mommy's going to jump in the water.'

"What can I do? My children are watching me. They're watching to see how I do it. How I deal with my fear. So I jump in."

I bought one of those blue ribbons at the store the other day. It has a dolphin on it with the words "Best Swimmer" printed in gold. I'm mailing it to my friend Carol for Mother's Day. I admire most moms, but I'm in awe of the ones willing to jump in feet first.

WHAT MY CHILDREN HAVE MADE ME

When Mother's Day approaches, I want to thank the three extraordinary human beings who have made me what I am today: my children. My children have made me crazy, they've made me cry, and some days they've made me wonder why they didn't come with a money-back guarantee. But mostly, they've made me a better person than I was before they wedged their way into my life and my heart.

I discovered, on my sixteenth Mother's Day, that most of what I really need to know about how to live, what to do, and how to be, I learned from my children. I garnered a wisdom not found in any textbook and skills not acquired on any job.

My children have taught me
- to never stop asking, "Why?"
- to skip instead of walk
- to let go of grudges, because the sun is shining, flowers are in bloom, and it's time to play
- how unimportant most things really are—especially dishes, laundry, and paperwork—when the sun is shining and flowers are in bloom
- how healing a hug can be, not only for the receiver, but also for the giver
- that a fistful of dandelions are more precious than a florist's finest roses
- how good it feels to giggle
- the total freedom in not caring what anyone thinks
- that it's okay to ask for help
- that it's fun to jump in mud puddles
- that you don't have to be perfect to be loved
- that regardless of what the mirror says, in their eyes, I am beautiful
- that we all need a nap every now and then
- that there's enough time in the day to examine rocks
- that sometimes you just have to be silly
- that hanging out with your best buds is still the best

I've discovered that in "raising my children up in the way they should go," it is I who have been risen.

In telling them to be kind, I have come away kinder.

In helping them to see the goodness in people, it is I who have had to reexamine my own relationships.

In teaching them to see the beauty in each day, it is I who have let myself see beauty.

In encouraging them to nurture their talents and follow their dreams, I've rediscovered my own, and as I reach for my goals, my own personal cheerleading squad is there cheer me on.

In teaching them about God, my own faith has been strengthened.

In telling them not be afraid, I have come away braver.

In accepting their shortcomings, I have learned to accept my own (most of them).

Through believing that my children can do or be anything, I have come to believe the same about myself.

Throughout these past sixteen Mother's Days, my children have made me Crayola drawings, lopsided clay pots, toothpick houses, burnt breakfasts in bed, and glittery greeting cards.

But mostly, they've made me more honest.

More trusting.

More alive.

More whole.

Yes, it's my children who have made me the woman I am today. And from what they tell me, they've done a pretty good job.

PUMPKIN FEST PHOOEY!

You can call me the Halloween Scrooge, but you won't find me at any pumpkin farm or pumpkin fest! Phooey! Whoever heard of such a thing? Cornstalk mazes, long food lines, petting zoos, CARNIVAL RIDES!

At Halloween? Why, in my day, a pumpkin WAS the fest. And we LIKED IT that way! Our pumpkin didn't come from any pumpkin patch, where you had to pay big bucks just to walk out in the field and cut it off the stalk yourself. We pulled it out of a pile at the grocery store. But we LIKED IT anyway!

And we stuck a real candle in it—not some cockamamie electric bulb. And it was a fire hazard and the pumpkin got soft and mushy and smelly fast. And we LIKED IT that way!

We didn't have any fancy costumes either. In my day, we wore PLASTIC! Plastic costumes that tied in back like hospital gowns. They came with plastic masks; we could hardly see out of.

They weren't safe. They weren't flame retardant. And we LIKED IT that way!

In my day, Mom never asked us what we wanted to be next year. We *knew* what we were gonna be next year. The same thing we were *last* year! Because those plastic costumes were indestructible. That costume is still hanging in my closet. And I still LIKE IT!

And kids didn't have any warm, toasty malls for trick-or-treating. In my day, we trick-or-treated outside in rain, freezing sleet, or knee-deep snow. And when it reached below zero, our tongues stuck to that little hole in our masks. And we couldn't even SAY trick-or-treat. But we LIKED IT anyway!

In my day, our parents didn't have time to take us on any hayrides or parties, because they didn't have any! And besides, they were too busy eating all of our Milky Way and Hershey Bars. And we . . . and we . . . HATED IT!

MASTERING THE ART OF GRAVY

"Taste it again," I pleaded with my sister. "Are you sure there isn't something missing? Salt? Pepper? Is it too thick? Too thin?"

My sister Jackie dipped her spoon into the hot, bubbly, brown liquid simmering atop the stove. Carefully raising it to her lips, she sipped tentatively and said, "It tastes great. Just like Mom's," she assured me. "Maybe better."

"Better? Don't say that!" I gasped, grabbing for the spoon. "There must be something wrong with it. I'm too young to make perfect gravy."

A somber mood enveloped me as I sat down to a dinner of medium-well roast beef (tinged with just the right touch of pink), buttery whipped potatoes with no discernible lumps, lightly seasoned corn, hot-buttered rolls, and, of course, rich, dark gravy to smother it all—as my husband would soon demonstrate with sheer delight.

My son, Marcus, would deposit his corn in the middle of his mashed potatoes before spooning on the gravy, a family tradition handed down for generations. It was a feast only my mother could make, but her daughter prepared this one.

I have survived my first turkey, pork roast, and chicken. I'm well beyond burning rolls and charring steak. I've prepared dishes my mother would never attempt and perfected the tried-and-true family favorites: peppered steak, pot roast, and pigs in the blanket.

My husband comes home and sniffs the aromas wafting through the kitchen with raised eyebrows—not with the Tums-bottle fear he'd had in my first few cooking years but with pure, anticipated, palatable pleasure. I possess the confidence and skill to prepare not only a passable feast, but also a memorable one. And a memorable meal in our family means you have reached the pinnacle of pan-gravy perfection. Yes, succulent gravy simmered in onions and turkey giblets marks the moving on of the next generation at the Thanksgiving table.

My first seat at any Thanksgiving table was at the kiddie table, where various-sized cousins tossed seeded rolls across a crowded room. I was oblivious to the two-day preparation going on in the kitchen and believed turkey and sweet potatoes, drenched in brown sugar, just magically appeared after the football game had ended.

Then I graduated to setting the table with Mom's white lace tablecloth and elegant silverware (reserved for holidays and out-of-town company), which was stored in the heavy oak box in the dining-room china cabinet.

The next year, I was promoted to stirring, mixing, and mashing duties, which included wiping the remnants of mashed potatoes off the counter, the wall, and, oops, Mom's new hairdo.

Once newly married, all that my new role required was to bring a dish of sweet potatoes to the yearly feast my mother prepared.

But now that I've mastered the art of adding salted potato water to the brown pan drippings with a mix of seasonings, and the exact, yet never measured, amounts of flour mixed together for proper thickening, Thanksgiving will be at my home.

It will be my bed piled high with coats. My home wafting with luscious aromas. My oven stuffed with a Butterball. My television blaring with the football game.

The responsibility and the praise of the meal will go to me.

And mom will sit, smiling proudly, watching and remembering as I season and stir the gravy.

THE FIRST THANKSGIVING

After years of feasting with loved ones on Thanksgiving, I can only imagine what it must've been like at that first Thanksgiving:

Two Days before the Holiday—at the Pilgrim Home

Wife:"You invited how many people to dinner?!"

Husband:"Honey, it's just our dear friend Chief Massosoit and a few of his family members."

Wife:"How many is a few? The chief has more cousins than God has sinners."

Husband:"I didn't get an exact count. What's the difference—eighty, ninety?"

Wife:"That's easy for you to say, John. You just stand out there in the field all day, watching the corn grow. I have to slave over a hot fire. I should've never agreed to come to this godforsaken land in the first place. But you made it sound so wonderful, with all that talk about the new cruise ship, the *Mayflower*."

Husband:"You saw the world, didn't you?"

Wife:"I can't remember. I was too busy throwing my guts for the entire cruise."

Two Days before the Holiday—at the Native American Tepee

Husband:"We're going where?"

Wife:"To the neighbors."

Husband: "But it's my day off. I just want to lie around the tepee all day. Besides, I don't want to eat with those people. They're so uptight."

Wife: "Well, you can offer it up this once. We haven't been invited to dinner in a hundred years."

Husband: "I'll tell you one thing: I'm not dressing up."

Wife: "Fine, wear whatever you want."

The Day before Thanksgiving

The chief and eighty-nine members of the Wampanoag tribe arrived at the Plymouth doorstep.

The Pilgrim women stood gaping, "Did our husbands tell you to come today? We're weren't expecting you until tomorrow."

The tribe trampled into the kitchen. "We brought you something," they announced while hoisting three deer and a dozen wild turkeys onto the kitchen table.

The Pilgrim men came into the kitchen and greeted their Indian friends: "Dudes! Let the party begin!" Then they went outside to play touch football.

As the Pilgrim women plucked the turkeys and skinned the deer, they mumbled under their breath:

"Couldn't they have just stopped at Baker's Square and picked up a pie?"

"And how about the chief? Dressed in nothing but a loin cloth!"

"Yeah, at least his wife could've told him to wear a tie."

Outside the men were having a grand time. The Pilgrims showed their new friends how to shoot muskets, and the Indians, in turn, showed them how to shoot a bow and arrow, until the women came running out and spoiled all the fun, "Give us those things, before somebody gets hurt!"

Then the men began beating drums wildly to entertain themselves before dinner, until the women came out, broke the drumsticks, and stuck the drums over their heads.

Finally, the feast was ready and everyone sat down to a bountiful harvest. The chief asked a Pilgrim child to lead the prayer.

"I don't know what to say," she admitted shyly.

"Just pray what you've heard your mother pray," the chief smiled encouragingly.

The little girl began, "Why in the Lord's name did my husband invite all these people to dinner?"

As the eating commenced, one happy Pilgrim hubby asked, "Who made the pudding? It's fantastic!"

"I did," the chief's wife replied.

"It's better than my wife's!" the Pilgrim husband shouted across the table.

Suddenly, a plop of pudding landed on his head.

One of the Indian men laughed. His wife gave him a good

nudge. His hand accidentally landed in the cranberries and it splashed out onto the Pilgrim's face across the table.

The food fight began in earnest. It lasted three days. Obviously, the Indians had never heard the oft-quoted English phrase, "If guests stay too long, they begin to smell like dead fish."

The next year, both families decided to stay home.

It wasn't until the following year that Thanksgiving was officially instated. However, it was distinctly written that the feast was only to last one day. And that's how our traditional feast began.

THE BIG TALK

There comes a time in all parents' lives, when they must face the "big talk." You know the talk I'm referring to, the one that starts with S!

The first problem with the "S talk" is exactly when to bring it up. Probably before your child hears it from his friends at school. But how would you know? A good indication is right after your kid gets pummeled on the playground.

To our dismay, some children find out on their own when they catch you in the bedroom in an uncompromising position. Others get hints from movies and the media, which are rarely helpful. I found out when my friend uncovered her parents' secret hiding place in the basement.

Blindly following in the footsteps of generations before them, some parents simply choose to ignore the S talk and never bring it up at all, convincing themselves that their kids will manage just fine without it.

But just because the wimpy way out worked for your parents, doesn't necessarily mean it will work for you.

So for those of you faced with the big talk this year, I'd like to be of some help. In my home, I found an effective way of handling a very delicate situation.

First, make sure your child cannot easily escape from the subject. Driving in a speeding car might work. But I suggest sitting down over a soothing mug of hot cocoa (yours is spiked, of course).

The parent begins first: "So, um, son, um, this is a special year for you, young fella—I mean little man; I mean young man. I believe that you're old enough, and hopefully mature enough, to know the truth about S . . . S . . . Santa Claus."

Of course, your son will roll his eyes, swig his hot cocoa in one gulp, and say, "I already heard it all at school. Not to mention that Sears sticker you left on my new bike last year. Oh, and I caught you and Dad in the bedroom wrapping up my Rollerblades. I know the truth about Santa Claus, Mom."

"Well, obviously you don't know enough to become an official member of the SSS?"

"The what?"

"The SSS: Secret Santa Society. An official deputy of Santa Claus himself."

"But there isn't a—"

"Shh! Don't ever say that!" I caution. "That's one of the rules of the special society. If you say there isn't a You Know Who, your membership is immediately revoked."

"Re-what?"

"Cancelled."

"Oh."

"It all began 1,600 years ago . . ."

"Wow, before you and Dad were born?"

"Uh, yeah. In a small seaport village in Greece. On December 6, a baby boy was born. His parents named him Nicholas. Now Nicholas had this ability to recognize people in need. And he grew up to be a very kind and caring person who often helped the poor. Nicholas never wanted the people to know where the help came from, so he often delivered gifts at night when everyone was sleeping. Once he even dropped gold coins down the chimney and they ended up in some stockings drying by the fire.

Throughout Nicholas's life, he helped so many people and followed his religion so faithfully that the Catholic Church declared him a saint."

"Okay, so . . . what does this have to do with Santa Claus?"

"I *am* talking about Santa Claus."

"Huh?"

"Saint Nick and Santa Claus are one in the same. After Saint Nicholas died, people from all over the world heard about his good deeds and decided to follow in his footsteps of selfless gift giving. Of course, over time, the image of St. Nick changed and eventually he transformed into the jolly old figure we know today. In other countries, they still celebrate St. Nick's Day on December 6. But in America, we decided that Santa delivered presents on Christmas Eve."

"So you see, my son, there really is a Santa Claus and his spirit lives on in the hearts of each and every person who believes in helping and giving to others."

"Now that you know the truth, it is your duty, as an official member of the SSS, to uphold the values of Santa and to keep the magic and wonder alive for the younger generations and the many generations to come. You must never disrespect his memory in front of kids from ages one to ninety-two. Do you understand?"

"I think so."

"Good. So this day, I send you forth to uphold and honor the spirit of Santa Claus and the magic and miracles of Christmas."

"What should I do first, Mom?" My awe-struck son asked.

"Your duties begin, my dear son, by wrapping this stack of presents for me. Now be off and be lively!"

(I love that part).

"BETTER NOT POUT" HAS KIDS STRESSED OUT

It's that wonderful time of year again, when all good parents tuck their tiny tots into bed, with visions of sugarplums dancing in their heads. Then, wagging a finger to their noses, we say in a sinister voice, "REMEMBER, HE'S SEES YOU WHEN YOU'RE SLEEPING!"

I look into my young daughter's eyes. They're aglow alright, with fear! I'll bet I turned those sugarplums right into prunes. But who am I to break an honored, family tradition? Up the block and down the block, in the city, the suburbs, or the rural areas, the Santa Threat can be heard round the world.

"He knows if you've been bad or good so be good for goodness sake!"

Besides, I need her to go to sleep so I can finish wrapping. And tomorrow morning, I'll need her to wake up early, so I can get to the post office before it gets busy, and I'll need her to stay up late for the Christmas choir at church tomorrow night.

So we sing it, we shout it, we whisper it, and we pout it.

As we drag our kids from store to store, shuffle them from party to party, ignore them one minute and put them on display in their holiday finery the next, we repeatedly warn that Santa is watching and they better be good!

And exactly what constitutes "good" is as mysterious and mind boggling as the fat man himself. This invisible gauge for goodness has all tots in a turmoil, wondering what specific indiscretion is enough to scratch them from the nice list and move them to the naughty.

Talk about holiday stress!

But we're so busy with our own tinsel-filled tensions that we hardly notice. Instead we invoke the Santa Threat and expect them to . . . be good. Be quiet. Be patient. Be happy. Be nice. Be generous, altruistic even. Basically, we expect them to be as angelic and sweet as Jesus Himself.

We toss our kids' comforting routines aside like Aunt Gertrude's fruitcake. We drag them to parties where they're expected to eat pâté instead of pizza. In order to check off one more thing on our to-do list, we keep them out way past their bedtimes and then are completely amazed when they suddenly suffer a meltdown in the middle of Kmart.

Our older children find it difficult to concentrate on homework. They can't comprehend all the fuss and the many hoops they watch their parents willingly jump through to make a merry Christmas. Then we take away a teen's last defense: baggy pants. We order him into turtlenecks and slacks and wonder why they can't just get along.

In lowering our own expectations for a picture-perfect holiday, maybe we need to give our kids a break too. Let's not set them up to fail. If we can maintain their routines as much as possible, bring along a "things-to-do" bag for long car and shopping trips, pack a PB and J sandwich for those times when a relative serves pâté, give them some space to just be themselves, and, above all, recognize when they've had enough, maybe Santa will be so tickled with us that he just might put something in our stockings too!

HAPPY HOLI-MOMENTS

My friend said aloud what I had been thinking for weeks now: "I can't wait until the holidays are over."

She felt guilty about admitting it and somewhat surprised by her own Grinchiness, especially since she remembers when her own mother had voiced those same words. She had been appalled and dismayed by her mother's attitude at such a special time of year. (She had been single, too.)

Oh, sure, she vowed to be different, but you know what happens when you declare that! Whenever you say, "will be different," as in, "My marriage *will be different*" "My labor and delivery *will be different*" or "My holidays *will be different*," you mean "better than everyone else's," and it won't be long before the universe brings you to your knees, forcing you to cry, "Uncle!"

After cooking one too many holiday dinners, shopping for one too many gifts (given to one too many ungrateful recipients), baking and burning one too many cookies, and writing and mailing one too many cards, my friend and I had become the Scrooges of the season.

Yes, we were Christmas curmudgeons, although we tried to hide it under brightly colored wrapping paper and more than a few glasses of wassail.

In our hearts, we knew we had much to be thankful for. But we wondered why counting our blessings, our healthy children, our warm homes, and our family and friends didn't seem to help at this hectic time of year.

We dutifully donned our Santa hats, wrapped gifts for the needy, and some for the greedy, even took our children caroling at an area nursing home, to find a meaning beyond the presents.

And all the while our deepest fear loomed, "Is it possible, that we can no longer experience the comfort and joy of the holidays now that we are the ones responsible for creating the comfort and joy?"

Even during church services I couldn't seem to stop the mental checklist: find dress shoes to match Lauren's velvet dress, check and see if Marcus has outgrown his slacks, buy a gift for the grab bag at work, mail packages to Uncle Tom and Grandma Rose in California . . .

I longed for another perspective to get through the hectic week ahead. And it finally came to me one morning, in the place from which all my great ideas seem to flow (the shower): a quote, first introduced to me in my early writing days, emerged from the soap bubbles.

"We do not remember days, we remember moments."

—Cesare Pavese

As my teacher had explained, when you write about your life, you don't write about a day in your life; you highlight and write about the memorable moments within that day.

A calmness washed over me. I felt an almost instant relief and release from the responsible, impossible task of a holiday. My friend and I had been building up to that one Currier and Ives picture-perfect day.

But there are no perfect days. Although there are, I believe, perfect moments.

No, the six-hour ride to Grandma's will not be a joyride, but I'm positive there will be a moment or two when an out-of-tune Christmas carol will ring through the car, sounding better to us than the Mormon Tabernacle Choir. Of course, the car will erupt into chaos again. But we had a moment.

When we finally arrive at Grandma and Grandpa's, there will be more frenzy and the cries of exhausted little children. But I'm longing for that moment when I hug my mother and know I am truly home. It will only be a moment, but I'm going to treasure it and capture it as if I had a camera, so I can play it again, in slow motion, during that next moment when our dog accidentally tips over her tree.

Maybe I'll even write the moment down. I'll include that time when, coming home after a hectic evening of shopping, I drove up to our house and noticed how the Christmas lights sparkled, and how I thought for just one moment how exquisitely beautiful our house looked.

Maybe I'll include that moment when my son kissed his little sister under the mistletoe, or that sixty seconds when our dog walked around in reindeer ears before he yanked the ears off his head and ate them, or that look of pure joy on my three year old's face when she made tracks with her boots across the first fallen snow.

I'll definitely include the quiet moment in the coffee shop, when I wrote these words, as the shoppers bustled in and out, Christmas songs played in the background, the coffee grinder whirred, and my pen flew across the page.

MY GROWN-UP CHRISTMAS WISH

When Santa comes down the chimney with a single bound, I am handing him my resignation without a sound.

Somehow I think this jolly old elf, will laugh when he reads it, in spite of himself.

For this kind, wise man will most certainly understand, why a mother might wish, for just one Christmas, to resign as a grownup and be a kid again—age 5 or 6 or 7 . . .

I want to wake up on Christmas morning and pad into the living room in my flannel, footed pajamas.

I want all my presents to be toys.

I want to gobble up all the chocolate in my stocking before breakfast and not even know what a calorie or a fat gram is.

I want to tap dance in my black patent-leathers, twirl in my red velvet dress, and wear soft-white tights instead of control-top pantyhose.

I want all my relatives to tell me that I'm beautiful and believe them.

I want to decorate the cookies with too many sprinkles and layers of frosting and eat them all before they cool.

I want to see a foot of freshly fallen snow as magical, not a messy nuisance.

I want to sneak a cone out of the pantry, dash outside, and fill it with the fresh white snow and think it's the best snow cone I have ever tasted.

I want to make a glittery card out of construction paper that says, "I love you,"—and not have to buy anything else—and know that my gift is seen as a present of perfection in all its imperfection.

I want to run around with my cousins, laughing and giggling, and feel sorry for the boring adults in the kitchen.

When I'm tired from all the festivities, I want to be lifted up and held in someone's arms until I'm ready to play again.

When it comes to Christmas carols, I want to shout them out with glee and not even know when I'm singing off key.

I want to be too innocent to realize that families fight and complain and talk behind each other's backs during the holidays.

I want to stare in awe at the baby in the manger and wonder at the immense love one baby could have for all the world.

I want to believe that all children are loved and wanted.

I want to believe that anything is possible and anyone can change.

I want to believe in the power of giving without conditions, loving without ultimatums, and living without fear.

So Santa, take my holiday to-do list, my calorie counter, my pantyhose, my great big grown-up worries and make me a kid again.

If you do, I do promise to share with you the best chocolate-chip cookies in the whole wide world. My mommy made them.

CUPID'S ARROW PIERCES MOM'S HEART

Now that I know the truth, I can't believe I could've been so blind. The telltale signs were there, if only I'd been brave enough to look. The extra attention he took in selecting his wardrobe, instead of the usual indifferent rummaging through his bureau. The new way he parted his hair. The frequent showers with scented soap. The sudden excuses he found for leaving earlier and earlier every morning. And his eyes, his beautiful blue eyes, darted, shifted, never meeting my own.

Neither a well-meaning neighbor nor an anonymous phone call revealed the betrayal. He told me himself, during dinner, while I was chomping on a carrot.

"I have a girlfriend," my son blurted out before convulsing into a fit of giggles.

"A WHAAAA HUH CHUH?!" I asked, spewing bits of shredded carrot.

"I can't tell you (giggle, giggle) her (giggle) name. But she's REAL pretty and she has long red hair."

"Some racy redhead, huh?" I huffed while cutting his meat into teeny-tiny bite-sized pieces.

"Mom," he moaned. "You don't have to cut my meat THAT small. Here," he said, grabbing the knife, "let me try it."

"No!" I screamed. "Mommy will do it for you." After all those years of devotion and adoration of his mother, he was in love with someone else, someone younger, prettier, most likely with a few freckles across the bridge of her little upturned nose.

I remember it as if it were yesterday. At the tender age of two, my son had professed his undying love and recklessly asked for my hand in marriage. At the mature age of four, upon discovering that I was already wed, he vowed to live with his father and me forever, that is, until Cupid's arrow pierced his nine-year-old heart.

"So," I asked as casually as possible, "where'd you meet her?"

"In school."

"How do you know she likes you?"

"I can tell by the way she smiles at me."

Ah, the smile. For some, it's a smile. For others, it's a quick punch in the arm on the playground, a tug on a ponytail during multiplication tables, or a note secretly slipped inside a backpack on the bus ride home. Nothing can compare to the thrill of first love.

In the days following his true confession, Marcus managed to wedge his girlfriend's presence into every conceivable nook and cranny of my breaking heart. The carefully drawn pictures, once created for me, now bore her name at the top in bright-colored markers. When she was absent from school, he moped around the house. He spent his hard-earned allowance on bubblegum baubles for his beloved and embedded her name in his peanut-butter sandwiches.

I painfully listened to his elaborate plan for professing his love to her.

"I'm going to give this note to Tommy to give to Susie to give to Joe to give Donna to give to her on the playground tomorrow and ask her to write back and tell me if she likes me."

Suddenly, I wanted to shout, "No! Don't do it, baby!" It was no longer my own feelings I fretted about but my son's. I had peeled his grapes and hot dogs, stopped him from darting into the street, and protected him from sunburn and frostbite. But the pain of Cupid's piercing arrow was one danger I could not protect him from.

When Marcus came home from school the next day, I tried to read his face for any signs. "Well," I finally asked, "how did it go? Did you give your note to You Know Who?"

"What note? Oh, that note. No, I didn't give it to her."

"Why not?" I asked confused by his nonchalance.

"Well, Mom," he said while dipping into the cookie jar, "I decided against it. I think I'm going to wait until I'm ten to have a girlfriend. Can I go over to Danny's house? We're going to trade basketball cards."

"Sure, son. Be back before dark. Watch for cars. Zip your coat. Wear your mittens. And don't talk to any girls—uh, I mean strangers—darling."

PANE DI PASQUA

Nonna kneaded dough into all kinds of bread: sweetbread filled with ricotta cheese; pizza bread; bread shaped like pinwheels, sprinkled with powdered sugar; and thick crusty bread, ideal for dipping in dark, red wine. But the bread I remember most is Nonna's Pane di Pasqua (Easter bread).

"Debbie!" she called to me one Easter Sunday, in her own unique jumbled combination of English and Italian. "Vieni Qua. Look. Pane di Pasqua, I made-a for you."

It was an Easter basket shaped out of dough and baked to a smooth, tan finish. The handle was molded from two pieces of dough wound together like a single braid in a young girl's hair. The basket bulged in front, as if it were carrying life. It was flat on the back side so that you could hang it on the wall or lay it on the table.

"Inside is a hard-cooked Easter egg," my mother-in-law explained. "She has made them every year, since I was a little girl. I tell her it's too much work. But she doesn't listen."

Nonna smiled at me, asking with her eyes, if I approved.

Cradling the beautiful creation in my hands, I sat speechless, awed once again by the handiwork of this remarkable woman. This was just one of the many gifts Nonna, my husband's grandmother, made "especially for me" in the few years I was privileged to know her.

The first gift was also a basket. Miniature baskets crocheted out of yarn, stiffened with starch, and filled with candy coated almonds were the highlight of my wedding shower.

When my husband, Tony, and I moved into our first apartment, Nonna presented us with a kitchen witch. "Buona fortuna (Good luck)," she said. Then she added something in Italian and everyone laughed.

"What did she say?" I asked.

"She thinks the witch is brutta," my sister-in-law interpreted. "Brutta means ugly."

With its crooked nose, deep-set eyes, and mischievous grin, it was and still is the ugliest kitchen witch I've ever seen. Since our first apartment, the brutta witch has dangled from the ceiling in every kitchen, showering us with much buona fortuna.

Nonna's intricately stitched satin bonnet, which once adorned our son's tiny head, has been carefully tucked away until the day when he will place it on his own child's christened crown. And whether it's a cold afternoon in January or a damp morning in May, I slip into the soft booties Nonna crocheted especially for me—and every other member of the family.

There were Christmas ornaments and tablecloths, baby bibs and baby blankets, all fashioned from her never-idle fingers.

When not creating, Nonna was cooking. Homemade pasta dough rolled out on a cookie sheet and raviolis pressed closed with a fork were just the beginnings of her sumptuous, bountiful meals.

Every Easter Sunday, her two daughters and their growing families would crowd into her little apartment and share the bread Nonna had blessed at the church on Holy Saturday. The Pane di Pasqua was the central part of the Easter-morning feast in Nonna's kitchen.

Years later, Nonna's daughters hosted the traditional holiday dinners. Of course, Nonna supervised. Then, after the meal, when other family members tarried around the table, Nonna slipped silently to her room, where she prayed for hours, her gifted hands cradling a worn, Italian prayer book.

Ten years ago, on Holy Thursday, the day Christians believe Jesus sat down to His last supper, the day He broke bread with His friends, Nonna died in her sleep. I imagine that Jesus had heard of Nonna's delicious Pane di Pasqua and longed to share it with her on the Resurrection Day.

This year, the bread will still grace our Easter table, thanks to Nonna's daughter, who learned at her mother's loving hand. And as I bite into the sweet, flavorful bread, I will think of Nonna and the Pane di Pasqua, the bread of life. "Happy are they who are called to His supper."

HOLIDAY GREETINS FROM THE DISANDRO FAMILY

Dear family and friends,

Thanks for those incredibly tedious, lengthy, rambling holiday letters bragging—I mean brimming—with news about your perfectly wonderful families.

I thought to myself, *What better way to get back at you—I mean, to connect with you—than with one of my own?*

It was a year of triumph and tragedy, a year of tears and laughter, in our warm, loving household. As a matter of fact, it was so dramatic and inspiring, NBC decided to buy the screenplay I wrote last month and will be making it into a movie of the week. Al Pacino will be playing my husband and one of those lovely ladies from *Friends* will be playing me. To our delight and surprise, our own children will play themselves, since all three passed the screen test with flying colors!

Our son, Marcus, is playing basketball again this year, and lo and behold, an NBA scout came to see him play last week and signed him for the 2018-19 season.

Our lovely daughter Lauren is still taking swimming lessons, and it's a good thing, too, or she wouldn't have been able to rescue that family of five when their boat overturned on Lake Michigan. She swam out ten miles and dragged them in one by one.

The Coast Guard planned to award her with a medal. But she refused, saying it was simply her civic duty. So her act of bravery shall forever remain a family secret.

Marcus was falsely accused of smuggling drugs in his lunch-box. What a horrific experience! It was the first time he had been called to the principal's office for something other than an academic-achievement award. Of course, the mistake was quickly corrected. But take my advice. Never put oregano in a little plastic bag to sprinkle over your child's pizza.

We almost lost our lives on our summer vacation in Florida. Our family became stranded at the top of a roller coaster, at a certain amusement park that shall remain nameless.

But my dear, courageous husband overcame his fear of heights and managed to climb down ten stories (it's a good thing he'd been lifting weights) and fix the mechanism before the rescue squad arrived.

On his way down, he resuscitated a lady in cardiac arrest and bandaged a man's badly twisted ankle. (Thank goodness for that first-aid class he took last spring). The media quickly got hold of it, but you know my husband—he's so modest. He refused to release his name or pose for photos, so it shall for-ever remain a family secret.

As for myself, I'm doing fine, although I almost died this fall during a major operation—the first of it's kind in the U.S. It's only been performed successfully in Sweden and Brazil on two other patients. The doctor's gave me a ten percent chance of survival. Great odds, huh? But I fooled them all. Before Christmas I was "walkin in a winter wonderland."

Despite the intense pain after the sixty-hour surgery, I managed to bake sixteen different kinds of Christmas cookies. Our home won Best-Decorated House in the Subdivision again this year. I'm surprised no one else thought of staging a live nativity scene. Sure, it was cold—especially with the forty-below windchill fac-tor, but we only suffered minor frostbite after our all-night vigil.

Well, another year has come to a close. And what an amaz-ing year it has been. It was so incredible that I can hardly believe it myself!

You are often in our thoughts and conversations (and if you only knew what we were saying about you).

Happy Holidays
from the DiSandro Family